SO...
YOU'RE THE NEW BAND DIRECTOR:
NOW WHAT?

PHILLIP C. WISE, PH.D.

FOREWORD BY
M. MAX MCKEE

D1598776

C.L. BARNHOUSE COMPANY
Music Publishers Since 1886 • P.O. Box 680
Oskaloosa, Iowa 52577 U.S.A.

Cat. #079-3009-00

SO...YOU'RE THE NEW BAND DIRECTOR: NOW WHAT?
Phillip C. Wise - 2nd Edition

C.L. BARNHOUSE COMPANY
Music Publishers Since 1886 • P.O. Box 680
Oskaloosa, Iowa 52577 U.S.A.

DEDICATION

To my wife, Linda, who truly understands life's struggles,
yet always remains optimistic.
Thanks for teaching me to smile!
And to my precious daughter Madison – a gift from God.

CONTENTS

PREFACE

Teaching is a wonderfully rewarding profession . . . it can also be difficult and overwhelming if you enter unprepared. Many new directors set foot in this arena wearing rose–colored glasses, uninformed of the realities, and unaware of the requirements. This book is intended to be a guide, a foundational approach to your first year in the field. It is written primarily for study during the undergraduate college experience and is especially useful to learners nearing their professional semester in preparation to student teach.

This text is divided into six sections that deal with the practical, pragmatic, technical, and philosophical elements of instrumental music education. Virtually every aspect needed to succeed during the inaugural year is addressed, from what to do prior to beginning the school year, to what to say on the first day of class, from building professional relationships, to rehearsal and performance techniques. The final section offers advice on how to formulate job application materials and successfully interview. In addition, you will find an extensive appendix which includes administrative forms, publisher listings, and professional organizations.

A heartfelt thanks to my former teachers, whose influences can clearly be seen in this writing: Edward L. Wingard, Ph.D., Tom Duden, Ed.D., David Evans, D.M.A., Paul Carpenter, D.A., and Bernard O. Onerheim. To my editor Shannon Vesely and production editor David Daniels – this experience would not have been possible without your assistance. Also a special thanks to my esteemed colleagues on the music faculty at Missouri Southern State College.

Go forth and succeed!

Phillip C. Wise

FOREWORD

As an individual launching a career in band directing, you are about to embark on the most amazing journey anyone could ever imagine. Band directing is in one instant completely exhilarating and in another totally frustrating. It is a job so filled with rewards, it is often difficult to fathom why minor incidents can cause a feeling of complete inadequacy. It is a profession in which learning new concepts is ever-exciting while serving as a needling reminder how ill-prepared we really are.

However, it is important to remember that band directing is first and foremost about people. If you like young people and care what happens to them, you are about to make a difference in the lives of countless individuals. Though you will pay a high price in terms of energy demands and required persistence, it will all come back to you tenfold every time you witness newfound confidence on the face of a student who learned something about music or something about life because of you.

There is little question but that band directing is one of the most complicated jobs man ever invented. Yet, at the same time, it is probably the only profession that develops qualities of total leadership and the complete understanding of complex organization. As a director you will be expected to prepare bands for concert, marching, and jazz performances while working one-on-one with students on more than a dozen entirely different instruments. At the same time you will deal with finances, promotion, publicity, travel arrangements and fundraising as well as show production and narration, equipment purchases and management, uniform design and maintenance, library and inventory, not to mention score selection and preparation, music arranging and marching band charting, private teaching and ensemble coaching, community service and festival preparation along with ever-present counseling and parenting.

Obviously, you didn't just close the cover of this book, deciding to explore a more mundane career. In any case, don't be discouraged by that rather overwhelming list of duties and responsibilities. The clear and concise presentation Dr. Phillip C. Wise has prepared for you in SO . . . YOU'RE THE NEW BAND DIRECTOR: NOW WHAT? will give you real insight into many important facets of band directing.

What Dr. Wise has included represents a synthesis of proven methods, materials and ideas. The many practical examples will provide you with a launching pad from which you can become airborne rather comfortably while learning how to handle the controls. If you are beginning with a good set of musical and people management skills, once you have extracted many of the ideas contained in this book to fit your situation and personality, you will not fail.

Couple all of that with the knowledge that there are thousands of us who have been in this business for thirty years or more who are willing to help smooth the way for you. So, share your dreams as well as your concerns with those who have already been on this most amazing journey. We know how it feels, and we never lose our willingness to help nor our love for a truly great profession.

M. Max McKee, Director
The American Band College
Editor, Bandworld Magazine

Whatever you vividly imagine,
ardently desire, sincerely believe,
and enthusiastically act upon . . .
must inevitably come to pass!

— Paul J. Meyer

PART ONE

BEFORE SCHOOL BEGINS

"Come to the edge," he said. They said, "We are afraid."
"Come to the edge," he said. They came. He pushed them
. . . and they flew.

– *Guillaume Appolinaire*

First Year Philosophy

In a short amount of time you will have survived the rigors of college, the struggles of preparing a resume, endured the interview process, and signed on the dotted line. SO . . . YOU'RE THE NEW BAND DIRECTOR: *NOW WHAT?*

The first year at any new job is a challenge. Expectations, relationships, rehearsals, performances, paperwork, and a host of other important issues face you. How will you approach your new position? Will you enter with great confidence, taking charge and implementing change immediately? Or will you use your first year to evaluate the situation while making plans for the following term? Perhaps you will take a middle–of–the–road approach, making a case by case evaluation as each situation presents itself. No one can tell you which method is best because each situation is dependent upon your philosophy, personality, school district, administration, community, and students. Don't be alarmed, there are ways to help ensure success!

The keys to a successful first year can be remembered by the acrostic **P.O.P – PREPARATION, ORGANIZATION,** and **PRECLUSION.** In truth, these skills define a master teacher. Will you make mistakes? Of course! Teachers are not perfect, nor will they ever be; however, with preparation, organization, and preclusion, you limit the majority of first year errors. It is also imperative that you be flexible and willing to adapt; after all, *the only thing constant in life is change.* Beginning right now, consider yourself a professional music educator, and although you may feel apprehensive about embarking upon this new chapter in your life, *take that monumental step to the other side of the podium.*

Discipline

Discipline must be dealt with *prior to beginning the school year.* This is your first task! Over the past ten years, public school systems have evolved into a virtual disciplinary nightmare. Recent studies show that one in ten public school students admits to bringing a gun to school, and one in fourteen discloses that they have been threatened by a gun. One hundred thirty–five thousand guns are brought to school every day! In addition, over nine hundred public school teachers are verbally abused every hour, and forty are physically assaulted in that same scant time frame. The fact that these major disciplinary issues exist is evidence that a host of less severe problems occur on a regular basis. Whether you believe this to be a societal problem or an educational one, you must be *ready and willing* to deal with the situation.

Let's first agree upon the correct definition of discipline. **Discipline is simple order** – nothing more and nothing less. *Without order, you have chaos.* Will you have discipline issues arise? Of course! All professional educators encounter them; however, it is the method in which you approach and deal with these issues that will allow you to succeed. Disciplinary responsibilities are inherent in your job description; you cannot simply transfer these adversities to your building principal. *You* will be responsible for handling the majority of classroom disruptions, so the quicker you sharpen your skills, the better.

Many educators have model classrooms, and no doubt you have experienced, first hand, a teacher who has demonstrated exemplary skills. By the same token, most have been exposed to a teacher who exhibited poor disciplinary methods, a situation where chaos was tolerated. The title of teacher not only brings *empowerment*, but *responsibility* – the responsibility to maintain an orderly and educationally sound environment for your students. Unfortunately, one of the most basic tools needed to survive in education is rarely discussed in college teacher preparation courses, and although your student teaching experience is a worthwhile endeavor, it does not authorize you to have complete disciplinary control. The three keys to a successful discipline plan are: **EXPECTATIONS, CONSISTENCY**, and **FAIRNESS.**

Expectations

Olympic gold medalist, Frank Shorter stated " . . . motivation is a subtle thing; there must be an *attainable goal* if one is to succeed." Disciplinary success begins with the development of high but attainable expectations. What kind of behavior should you require of your student musicians? Only you can answer that question. Of special consideration is the fact that instrumental groups tend to be much larger in size than traditional classrooms, sometimes housing three or four times as many learners. This, coupled with the fact that all of your students have access to *noisemakers*, demands that your expectations be very high.

Take time to list your behavioral expectations.

1. _____

2. _____

3. _____

4. _____

5. _____

6. _____

7. _____

8. _____

9. _____

10. _____

Now that you have a list in place, work to clarify your expectations by meticulously wording them as short, concise statements. For example, if your rule is no talking unless you raise your hand, clarify by stating: no talking unless you raise your hand and are recognized by the teacher. This discourages students from simply raising their hand and blurting out a comment. The clarification states that they must not only raise their hand, but must be *recognized* by the teacher before speaking. If you have two objectives that are similar, combine them to cover both areas.

Take your five primary behavioral expectations (rules) and carefully articulate them below.

1. _____

2. _____

3. _____

4. _____

5. _____

Consistency

As difficult as this may be, even for the experienced teacher, *you must be consistent*! Consistency is defined as a compatibility among parts, a degree of firmness. If you expect your discipline plan to be effective, you must assert this type of balance. If you are not consistent with your rules, consequences, and rewards, *you will fail*.

One of the more difficult concepts for the new educator to grasp, is the fact that students *expect* consistent discipline from their teachers. Sure, some may grumble about your policy and parents may complain as well; however, it is your obligation as a professional educator to remain *consistent* once you have stated your expectations. If you allow Randy to escape the consequence for breaking a rule that you reprimanded James for, then you have failed in this area. It will be virtually impossible to build or regain student respect following an episode like this.

Complications can surface during the inaugural year because students and parents test new teachers and their policies. Additional difficulties can arise when you must discipline children of colleagues or community socialites. This can be especially troublesome if you are in a small town, as the rumor mill is always operating at full force. Nevertheless, you must treat these students as you do all others. Without consistency, your discipline policy will fall short because your students will view you as a biased teacher who shows favoritism.

Fairness

Does the consequence fit the broken rule? Is it just and equitable? Students will keep a watchful eye to see if you are a *fair* disciplinarian. Some teachers allow their students to assist in establishing rules and consequences for the class in hopes that they will then be perceived as impartial. Although this may work for some educators and in some situations, it is best not to empower students with this administrative responsibility. A few would argue that student ownership of the discipline plan fosters adherence; however, such rationale has not been proven. As the instructor, you must establish fair rules and consequences.

Use common sense! If a student breaks your rule of no talking without raising their hand and being recognized, it would be unjust to dismiss them from band for this first offense. List five consequences of increasing severity you believe to be fair and objective.

1. _____

2. _____

3. _____

4. _____

5. _____

Rules and Consequences

Keep your rules to no more than six with the same number of consequences. Be sure they are posted in the front of the room for all to see. The following is an example of rules and consequences appropriate for the middle school/junior high or high school level.

Rules

1. No talking while rehearsal is in progress
2. Raise your hand and be recognized by the teacher before speaking
3. Have appropriate materials in class
4. No food or drink in the bandroom
5. Keep your hands and feet to yourself

Consequences

1st Offense	Verbal Warning
2nd Offense	One night detention
3rd Offense	Two nights detention and meeting with parent(s)
4th Offense	Dismissal from band until meeting with parent(s) and principal
5th Offense	Dismissal from band for one quarter (nine week period)

You must also include a severe discipline clause in your policy. This statement declares that in the event a student blatantly and/or maliciously causes a serious classroom disruption, the severe disciplinary clause will supersede all other consequences and the student will immediately be taken to the principal's office, and serve the fourth offense consequence.

Positive consequences should also be included in your discipline model. It is important to reward appropriate behavior as this builds influence with other students, decreases the amount of problem behavior, and makes for a more positive classroom environment. The following is a list of possible rewards.

• Personal attention from the teacher

• Positive notes to parent(s)

• Special awards designed by the teacher and/or students

• Special privileges

• Material rewards

• Home rewards in collaboration with parent(s)

• Group rewards when the entire ensemble meets a goal

Not all of your students and their parent(s) will wholeheartedly agree with your disciplinary ways. Some may object and, on occasion, confront you. If this happens, remember that *you* are the teacher, *you* are the director, *you* are the single person in charge of *your* class. Let the parent(s) verbalize their concern, but under no circumstance should you allow them to influence or alter *your* approved discipline policy.

Can you have strong classroom discipline, retain a sense of humor, and be a sensitive and caring teacher? Of course! Just because you expect your discipline policy to be followed does not mean you will be labeled a tyrant or that your students will hate you. On the contrary, with established disciplinary groundrules in place, you and your students are freed from the constant uneasiness of what might happen and how you will respond. Remember, *discipline is simple order*, nothing more and nothing less.

Band Handbook

Have your band handbook ready to be passed out to your students on the first day of class. What is a band handbook? This is a document presented to your students and their parents which contains band policies, regulations, schedules, and other important information. By presenting a handbook, you *preclude* numerous problems, and preclusion is a necessity during your first year. If a handbook already exists, carefully review it, making needed alterations prior to seeking support and approval from your administrator.

Before you begin drafting your handbook, solicit applicable district and board policies from your administration. These may include procedural items, district grading methods, discipline structures, transportation guidelines, etc. By including these procedures as a foundation for your own policies, you build a uniformed base with district and building statutes, thus creating instant administrative support. For example, if the district behavior plan states that after school detention can be given if the student verbally receives a one day notice, then include this in your policy.

Your handbook need not be long; the shorter and more concise you make it, the better. Once you have drafted the document, schedule a meeting with your principal to discuss implementation. Request that your principal sign the welcome page. This serves as documented support and approval of the contents. Most administrators will be pleased that you have taken the time to outline important information regarding your program and will offer their assistance.

The following is an example of a handbook contents page.

I.   Cover Page
II.   Table of Contents
III.   Welcome Letter
IV.   Policy Statement
V.   Philosophy of Music
VI.   General Information
       a. Marching Band
       b. Concert Band
       c. Jazz Ensemble
       d. Pep Band
       e. Uniforms
       f. Instructional Lessons
       g. Auditions
       h. Equipment Needs
VII.   Transportation Policy
VIII. Grading Policy
IX.   Discipline Policy
X.   Music Calendar
XI.   Acknowledgment Form

Cover Page: Include school name, academic year, your name, and table of contents.

Welcome Letter: Write a positive, informative, and grammatically correct letter. Be sure to include a welcome and personal introduction, outline the contents of the handbook, and make reference to the acknowledgment form requesting a parental signature. Your principal should sign this letter in support.

Policy Statement: Seek any district policy statements that are mandatory when distributing formal documents to students and/or parents.

Philosophy of Music: Compose a short and concise philosophy statement (one or two paragraphs).

General Information: Give a brief overview of the instrumental music program which may include the following: marching band, concert band, jazz ensemble, pep band, uniforms, instructional lessons, auditions, and equipment needs. Additional information may be included in this section depending upon special needs or circumstances.

Transportation Policy: Follow the district's policy when presenting this aspect of the handbook.

Grading Policy: List your grading scale, weighting system, and measurable objectives.

Discipline Policy: Specifically outline all aspects of your discipline policy (some prefer to use the word behavior as opposed to discipline as it takes away any negative connotations).

Music Calendar: List all concerts and outside rehearsals for the entire year. Suggest that parents post this schedule in the home for quick reference.

Acknowledgment Form: Request that students and parents sign and return this page of the handbook. This form acknowledges that this information has been received.

The following sample handbook includes each of these primary components.

Royal Heights High School

Band Handbook

199_ – 199_

Welcome Letter
Policy Statement
Philosophy of Music
General Information
Transportation Policy
Grading Policy
Discipline Policy
Music Calendar
Acknowledgment Form

Mr. Bradley A. Johnson

Director of Bands

Royal Heights High School Band

Bradley A. Johnson
Director of Bands

August 29, 199_

Dear Parent(s)/Guardian(s) and Student:

Greetings! I trust you had an enjoyable summer and are looking forward to the upcoming school year. I take this opportunity to introduce myself and invite you to join our Band Booster organization which meets the first Tuesday of every month at 7:30 p.m. in the bandroom.

In our handbook you will find policies, procedures, and other important information regarding the Royal Heights High School Band Program. Please take the time to read this material, as the success of our band depends upon each individual working toward the same goals. Sign the acknowledgment form and have your child return it to me by September 4, 199_.

If you have questions, feel free to contact me at school.

Sincerely,

Bradley A. Johnson
Director of Bands

Thomas E. Davis
Principal

ROYAL HEIGHTS POLICY STATEMENT

It is the policy of the Royal Heights School District that the curriculum content and instructional materials utilized reflect the cultural and racial diversity present in the United States and the variety of careers, roles, and lifestyles open to women as well as men in our society. One of the objectives of the total curriculum is to reduce stereotyping and to eliminate bias on the basis of sex, race, ethnicity, religion, and physical disability. The curriculum should foster respect and appreciation for the cultural diversity found in our country and an awareness of the rights, duties, and responsibilities of each individual as a member of a multicultural, multiethnic, nonsexist society

PHILOSOPHY OF MUSIC

Every aspect of music is important and will be emphasized at various stages in a student's development. The core of the instrumental program is the symphonic concert band. From this ensemble, groups such as the marching band, jazz ensemble, pep band, and various chamber groups are derived. The Royal Heights music department stresses the advancement of the student's abilities to function in both the large group and small ensemble setting. Music offers a unique opportunity to challenge each student cognitively, affectively, and physically. It provides for emotional expression, intrinsic worth, and has a positive impact on individuals, families, communities, and cultures.

GENERAL INFORMATION

Marching Band: Marching band is open to all band members in grades 9 - 12. The band performs at pregame and halftime during each home football game and marches in two area parades. Early rehearsals are held every Tuesday and Thursday during marching season at 7:00 a.m.

Concert Band: The concert band is open to all band members in grades 9 - 12. The band rehearses first period (8:30 - 9:20) daily. The season begins in November following the last home football game. Specific concert dates are listed on the attached music calendar.

Jazz Ensemble: Membership is open to all high school students who qualify by audition. Auditions are held in late November and rehearsals are then held Monday, Wednesday, and Friday mornings 7:00 - 8:20. The jazz ensemble performs three formal concerts and participates in two area festival/clinics.

Pep Band: All band members participate in pep band. Two bands will be assembled based on instrumentation needs and will perform at all home basketball games. The performance schedule will be distributed in October.

Uniforms: The school will provide all concert and marching uniforms with the exception of band shoes. These must be purchased through the Royal Heights Band Boosters at a cost of $29.95.

Instructional Lessons: All band members receive one instructional group lesson per week. Schedules will be posted in the bandroom during the first week of school.

Auditions: Auditions for chair placements are held twice each school year (September and January). Specific requirements and procedures are posted in the bandroom.

Equipment Needs: Each learner must bring to class everyday: a sharpened pencil, a notebook of paper, their instrument (excluding percussionists) in good working condition, assigned music, and a good attitude.

Transportation Policy: It is the policy of the Royal Heights School District that all band members ride school transportation to away events. Students may ride home with parents or a relative providing they have submitted the transportation release form **prior** to leaving for the event. This form is available from the director.

GRADING POLICY

Weighting

Rehearsals   33%
Performances   34%
Instructional Lessons 33%

Rehearsal Criteria (weekly grade)

- Student on time for rehearsal
- Instrument and appropriate materials
- Attentive and exhibiting good conduct
- Attendance to all rehearsal sessions
- Performing music at a proficient level

Performance Criteria (grade for each performance)

- Student on time for performance warm-up
- Instrument and appropriate materials
- Attentive and contributing to a good performance
- Individual part performed at a high level of proficiency

Instructional Lessons (weekly grade)

- Attendance to all required lessons
- Practice goals were met (180 minutes per week)
- Lesson material performed at a high level of proficiency

Grading Scale

A	96-100
A-	90-95
B+	87-89
B	83-86
B-	80-82
C+	77-79
C	73-76
C-	70-72
D+	67-69
D	63-66
D-	60-62
F	0-59

DISCIPLINE POLICY

In order to maintain an orderly educational environment, the following discipline policy will be implemented.

Rules

1. No talking while rehearsal is in progress
2. Raise your hand and be recognized by the teacher before speaking
3. Have appropriate materials in class
4. No food or drink in the bandroom
5. Keep your hands and feet to yourself

Consequences

1st Offense	Verbal Warning
2nd Offense	One night detention
3rd Offense	Two nights detention and meeting with parent(s)
4th Offense	Dismissal from band until meeting with parent(s) and principal

5th Offense   Dismissal from band for one quarter (nine week period)

Positive consequences will vary each semester.

SEVERE DISCIPLINE CLAUSE

In the event a student blatantly and/or maliciously causes a serious classroom disruption, the severe disciplinary clause will take effect and the student will immediately be taken to the principal's office, and will serve the fourth offense consequence.

This discipline policy has been approved by the School District Administration.

MUSIC CALENDAR
(place on separate sheet)

Date	Event	Meeting Time
September 7	Marching Band Performance	6:45 p.m.
September 14	Marching Band Performance	6:45 p.m.
September 18	Marching Band Pictures	8:30 a.m.
October 12	Marching Band Performance	6:45 p.m.
October 19	Marching Band Performance	6:45 p.m.
October 27	All-State Auditions	7:00 a.m.
November 9	Pancake Day Parade - Centerville	8:30 a.m.
December 8	Concert Band Holiday Concert	8:30 p.m.
December 10	Concert Band BCRH Concert	7:00 p.m.
December 12	Jazz Ensemble Concert	7:00 p.m.
December 14	Jazz Ensemble Concert - Mall	1:30 p.m.
January 23	MSSC Jazz Festival	8:00 a.m.
January 28	SMU Honor Band Festival	7:00 a.m.
February 26	Concert Band Winter Concert	7:00 p.m.
March 8	Tri-State Jazz Festival	8:00 a.m.

March	20	State Solo/Ensemble Contest	7:00 a.m.
April	10	Concert Band Fun Night Concert	7:00 p.m.
May	7	State Large Group Contest	5:00 p.m.
May	14	Concert Band Spring Concert	7:00 p.m.
May	16	Jazz Ensemble Concert	7:00 p.m.
May	28	Concert Band - Commencement	1:00 p.m.
May	29	Tulip Festival Parade - Pella	9:00 a.m.

- *The pep band schedule will be distributed in October.*

- *Students will be notified in advance of any schedule changes.*

ACKNOWLEDGMENT FORM
(place on a separate sheet)

I acknowledge that I have received the 199_ - 199_ Royal Heights Band Handbook.

_____

Parent(s)/Guardian(s)   Date

_____

Parent(s)/Guardian(s)   Date

_____

Student   Date

This form is due Thursday, September 4, 199_.

Initial Meeting With Administration

Your objective in requesting this meeting is to secure administrative support and approval of your band handbook. This conference should be friendly, yet businesslike and your dialogue of collegial fashion, not the student/teacher relationship you may be accustomed to. It is crucial that you enter into this new association as a partner in the educational process. The following outline offers only a general approach to this meeting as the conversation may progress in any number of directions.

I.   **Welcome**

    a.   Proclaim your excitement in being a part of the faculty. State that you are looking forward to the coming school year.

    b.   Engage in some small talk, perhaps summer vacations, the weather, hobbies, etc.

II.   **Band Handbook**

    a.   State that you have been familiarizing yourself with district policies and have drafted a handbook which outlines band procedures and guidelines (discipline, grading, etc.).

    b.   Briefly outline the handbook and invite your principal to read the document and offer comments or suggestions. Request his/her support.

    c.   Discuss the handbook and answer all questions in a clear, precise, and honest manner; don't be defensive.

III.   Conclusion

      a.   Schedule a follow-up session.

      b.   Thank your principal for the meeting and reassure him/her that you are excited to *be on board.*

      c.   State that you look forward to your next visit.

During your follow-up meeting, be flexible and open to your administrator's suggestions. When administration have ownership in a project, they are more apt to approve it. Continue to present revised drafts until full support is rendered and then ask your administrator to sign the letter page. State that the signature lends credence to the contents. If he/she declines to sign, but will verbally support the document, write the following memorandum and send it the next day. Rule of thumb: keep a copy of all correspondence sent to and received from administration, parents, and students.

TO: Thomas E. Davis
FROM: Bradley A. Johnson *(your initials)*
DATE: August 12, 199_
RE: Band Handbook

This memo is to confirm our communication of August 11, 199_. We discussed the contents of the handbook and agreed that the document will be supported by the Royal Heights Administration. Your input into its design was most helpful. Thank you for your verbal endorsement.

If for any reason your administrator is not willing to support the concept of your handbook, make every attempt to find out why (although you may never really know). If you receive a pessimistic response, you have three options: continue plans to implement the document; seek the council of higher administration; or terminate the idea altogether. If you decide to continue implementation, tread lightly, for you have no administrative support system to fall back on. If you consult a higher ranking administrator, you may be viewed as a trouble maker, a rebel without sufficient cause. If you terminate the handbook idea, seek approval from your administrator to extract and retain your behavior and grading policies. Evaluate all aspects of this situation carefully before making a decision.

First Purchases

If your bandroom is not equipped with a large bulletin board, this should be your first purchase. A 4′ x 3′ enclosed plexiglass board with prefab letters not only looks professional but serves a most important purpose. *Post every upcoming event for the entire semester on this board* and place it in the front of the room where it can be seen by all. This display not only assists your learners with scheduling performance and rehearsal times but curtails those two irritating questions, "When is our next concert?" and "You didn't tell us about that!" With this information posted, students will quickly discern that you expect them to be responsible for keeping abreast of scheduled events.

An example of a bulletin board posting.

Date		Event	Meeting Time
September	7	Marching Band Performance	6:45 p.m.
September	14	Marching Band Performance	6:45 p.m.
September	18	Marching Band Pictures	8:30 a.m.
October	12	Marching Band Performance	6:45 p.m.
October	19	Marching Band Performance	6:45 p.m.
October	27	All-State Auditions	7:00 a.m.
November	9	Pancake Day Parade - Centerville	8:30 a.m.
December	8	Concert Band Holiday Concert	6:30 p.m.
December	10	Concert Band BCRH Concert	7:00 p.m.
December	12	Jazz Ensemble Concert	7:00 p.m.
December	14	Jazz Ensemble Concert - Mall	1:30 p.m.

If it is not possible for the school district to purchase this item, large white poster boards with information written in black marker will suffice. The boards should then be posted in front of the room at an elevated level for all to see. It is best not to use a section of the chalkboard to list these events as students have been known to erase and alter dates and times. Having to rewrite this information even once is simply poor time management.

The second item of purchase should be a repair kit. Although you may not have had any formal training in instrument repair, emergencies will arise (i.e. replacing the proverbial pad five minutes before a concert). These small repair kits can be purchased from a music store and will usually include various sized pads, string, razor blades, a small screwdriver set, rawhide hammer (good for almost anything), and other often needed repair items. Be sure to keep extra reeds, valve oil, and a mouthpiece puller in the kit as well.

Your third purchase should be three dozen thank–you cards. Place these in the top right hand drawer of your desk. When your booster group organizes a soup supper, send each person who assisted a thank–you note. When the custodian sets up the stage for your concert, send a thank–you note. When your administrator attends your first concert, send a thank–you note. This simple gesture takes very little time and will only enhance your public and professional relations.

PART TWO

DAY ONE

The difference between failure and success is doing a thing nearly right and doing a thing exactly right.

– Edward Simmons

ATTITUDE

The longer I live, the more I realize the impact of attitude on life. Attitude, to me, is more important than facts. It is more important than the past, than education, than money, than circumstances, than failures, than successes, than what other people think or say or do. It is more important than appearance, giftedness, or skill. It will make or break a company . . . a church . . . a home. The remarkable thing is we have a choice every day regarding the attitude we will embrace for that day. We cannot change our past . . . we cannot change the fact that people will act in a certain way. We cannot change the inevitable. The only thing we can do is play on the one string we have; and that is our attitude . . . I am convinced that life is 10% what happens to me and 90% how I react to it.

— Charles R. Swindoll

PROFESSIONALISM

Is teacher professionalism still in vogue? All too often emphasis is placed on what one can get *out of the job* rather than what one can put *into the job*. In short, professionalism is the appropriate combination of ethics, values, strategies, and philosophies. What specific qualities do all professionals possess? The following list highlights these important traits.

Pros love problems. While nonprofessionals whine and worry, professionals look forward to using their problem-solving abilities. Pros batten down problems; they cannot wait to tackle them.

Pros are punctual. They know that time is the most valuable of all commodities. Pros show up for class and meetings on time, deliver work on time, and respect the time of others.

Pros are reliable. They never pass the buck or resort to alibis; they simply do what is necessary to complete the job, even if obstacles stand in their way. They are always ready to figure out *another way* to accomplish the assignment. Their minds are disciplined, detail-oriented, and task-centered. They think in terms of specifics and substance, rather than empty generalities, and substantiate all judgments with facts and logic.

Pros are discerning. They do not hit tacks with sledgehammers; rather they take care to distinguish between major and minor problems. They boil down situations to their essence and take decisive action quickly, without agonizing.

Pros are organized. They have "TO DO" lists with them at all times, as well as a calendar and a notebook for recording ideas and observations as they occur. They have a simple and effective system for storing information.

Pros read avidly. They always have a book or professional journal on hand. They set priorities, reading the most useful material first.

Pros communicate well. Besides knowing how to speak, write, and listen well, they are sensitive and look for the little hints that help them understand the people around them. They know what to do and say in any given situation. They work on their communication shortcomings.

Pros are optimistic. They abhor negative thinking, and inspire others to have a positive attitude. They prefer to look for solutions, rather than to dwell on the problem.

Pros do not procrastinate. Because pros are confident, they don't put projects off. They will get started on a job even if they know in advance they don't have enough time to complete it that day.

Pros know their weaknesses. They compensate for them by seeking advice when necessary and giving themselves extra time on projects that draw on their less-developed skills. Since they are aware of interdependence, pros are quick to praise the accomplishments and abilities of others. Stroking comes naturally to them.

Pros cultivate their appearance. Pros know that first impressions are based on outward appearance, so they are careful about their image. They are neither flamboyant nor boring, but tend to be dressed a bit more conservatively than the person they are dealing with. They have charisma, based on the pattern of success.

Pros belong to professional organizations. Attending professional seminars and conferences are annual events as pros seek the latest research and teaching techniques in order to hone their craft.

Reprinted with permission from the *Mutualog*, Security Mutual Life Nebraska. Original source unknown.

OPENING REMARKS

The way you approach your first day will set the educational tone for the remainder of the year. The key is *preparation*. Stand in front of a mirror and record (on tape) your opening day speech. Just as you have practiced your instrument all of these years, you must now rehearse and evaluate your opening remarks. Write your name on the board (Mr. Mrs. Ms. _____) prior to the beginning of class, have adequate handout materials ready to be distributed, and present yourself as a confident and skilled music educator. If you get nervous and have butterflies, you are normal. Have a glass of water with you, take a few deep breaths, and speak at a calm articulate pace. The following outline simulates the first day of class.

I.   **Welcome**

    a. Welcome
    b. Roll call
    c. Short history about yourself
    d. Goals for the year

II. **Band Handbook**

    a. Pass out handbook
    b. Explanation of handbook contents
    c. Student questions regarding the handbook
    d. Explanation of bulletin board
    e. Fill out and collect identification cards
    f. Pass out health information forms (secondary level)

III. **Rehearsal**

(Don't push too quickly to rehearse during the first day. You will be much better off taking the entire period to clearly explain all band policies and procedures)

a. Warm up
h. *School Song*
c. *Star Spangled Banner*

The 3″ x 5″ identification cards mentioned in the outline are used to record general information about each student. A sample is shown below.

IDENTIFICATION CARD

Name _____

Address _____

Parent(s)/Guardian(s) Name _____

Home Phone _____   Secondary Phone _____

Grade _____ Age _____ Instrument _____

Years Played _____ Lesson Book _____

Private Study _____ yes _____ no

Additional Information:

If you plan to schedule out-of-town performances, you will need proper student health information. Distribute health registration forms and require your students and their parents to complete the questionnaire. Once you have collected these, place them in a three-ring binder and carry them with you whenever your ensemble is performing at an out-of-town event. Should a student health emergency arise, you can then quickly pass this information on to the attending physician. This precautionary measure just makes good sense, and it could save a life.

STUDENT HEALTH REGISTRATION

Student Name _____ SS# _____

Address _____ Date of Birth _____

Contact Person Name _____

Contact Person Address _____

Describe the following: (use back page if necessary)

recent illness _____

chronic or long-term illness _____

allergies _____

medicines currently being taken _____

other medical or physical restrictions _____

_____

_____

_____

Parent or Guardian Consent Statement

I grant permission for the above named person to be treated and/or hospitalized by a licensed physician if an emergency situation arises.

SIGNED: _____ DATE: _____

WORK PHONE: _____ HOME PHONE: _____

Project an Image

We know that professionals take pride in their appearance and image. As an educational leader, you have only one chance to make a positive first impression on your students. Dress conservatively! Men should wear a sports suit, tie, and dress shoes, and ladies, a dress or pant outfit and dress flats. As the year progresses and a rapport has been established, you may wish to *loosen-up* and dress more casually. The first few months of formal dress is not intended to create a false impression, but to create the proper image: that of a leader. Executing this leadership role can be a challenge for young directors and is often exacerbated by the close proximity in age between teacher and high school student. If you want to be treated like a professional, begin by dressing like a professional.

There will be times during the year that will call for a more casual look. Rehearsing a high school marching band is one example, especially if your style is a *hands on – how to* approach. Performances such as halftime shows, parades, and pep band also require special consideration. During these events you are being observed by the community, parents, administration, and students. Always represent yourself and your band with pride and dignity.

DISCIPLINING THE FIRST OFFENDER

When presenting your discipline policy, be very *matter of fact* in your approach. Making light of the issue sends the wrong message: *you don't have to take me seriously.* Humor is a wonderful tool which can accomplish many things; however, this is simply not the time or place. An improper delivery can be lethal.

Once you have stated your discipline policy, offer a short question and answer time. If there are no questions, restate the query, "Is there anyone who did not fully understand my discipline policy?" Don't belabor this point; state your question and move on to the next item of business. When the first offender breaks a rule, and there will always be one student who will test you (usually only a few minutes following your well prepared oration), you must *walk your talk*. Under no circumstance allow the first offender to escape your stated consequence. This will open a can of worms that will be almost impossible to close.

When the inevitable transgression occurs, respond in a serious and expedient manner. "Robert, you just broke rule number one (no talking while rehearsal is in progress). Consider this a verbal warning," and go right on with class. If Robert chooses to break the rule again, in a more serious tenor, state, "Robert, you just broke rule number one again, the second consequence is one night detention, I will see you at 3:00" and continue with your class. Should Robert make argumentative comments, attempt to explain his actions, or make a scene, inform him that you understand what he is saying, and that he just broke rule number one for the third time and will now serve two nights detention. Don't get into an argument with Robert, or any student, for *you cannot win* when this occurs. Simply state the consequence and proceed with your teaching duties. If Robert persists, remove him from the room using the severe discipline clause and deal with the situation following class. You cannot allow any student to disrupt the learning environment.

By following through with your stated consequences, you will have proven yourself as a professional who is *consistent* with their discipline policy. This initial test will pave the way for the remainder of the year provided you continue to follow your established requisites. If, on the other hand, you choose to ignore Robert's talking in hopes that it will somehow magically disappear, you will be sadly mistaken. It will not go away and will only get worse. You will most likely find your next few rehearsals out of control. Why? By not being consistent, you made a clear statement: *it is all right to break my rules, for there are no consequences*. Face your first offender(s) assertively!

First Rehearsal

Your first playing rehearsal will most likely occur during your second class session, and you must be *prepared and organized.* Have music, flipfolders, stands, percussion assignments, instruments, seating arrangements, and all other details in order. Begin this rehearsal in the same manner that you plan to commence concert band sessions. This will assist in making a smooth transition following marching band season. Prepare a detailed lesson plan and spend the period indoors sightreading music for your upcoming performances.

This rehearsal will give you a good sense as to the musical strengths and weaknesses of your ensemble. It will also provide your students with a clear representation of your rehearsal style and musical expectations. If you are disorganized, searching for music, and unsure of your goals, you have delivered another nonverbal message to your students: *they need not be prepared.* Master teachers lead by example. The following is a sample outline for this all-important rehearsal.

I. **Warm Up (5 - 7 minutes)**

   a. List rehearsal order on board
   b. Warm-up concert Bb scale, concert F scale (rhythm variations)
   c. Chorale #1 - Clark warm-up book
   d. Tuning, beginning with low brass/woodwinds moving to higher pitched instruments, tune by chords

II. **Announcements (5 minutes)**

   a. Uniform checkout times
   b. Music needs to be memorized for first performance
   c. Announce drum major and percussion section leader responsibilities

d. Collect acknowledgment forms - due Wednesday
　　e. Collect health registration forms - due Wednesday

III. **Rehearsal (remainder of period)**

　　a. Rehearse – *Star Spangled Banner*
　　b. Rehearse – *School Song*
　　c. Rehearse – *Alabama Jubilee*
　　d. Rehearse – *My Favorite Things*

PART THREE

SCHEDULING & POLICIES

Do your work with your whole heart and you will succeed – there's so little competition.

– Elbert Hubbard

LESSON PLANS

As with most other aspects of the profession, preparation, organization, and preclusion equals success. Lesson plans allow you to prepare your long and short term goals, activities, and evaluations. When setting long term goals, your objectives may look something like this.

Broad Objective: Holiday Concert – December 8, 199_

October 10	Select seven concert band pieces for consideration
October 12	Begin serious score study
October 24	Concert Band rehearsals begin
October 24-31	Sightread and select five performance pieces
November 1	Rehearse through December 5th
December 6	Preconcert performance for Royal Heights Elementary Band
December 7	Dress rehearsal on stage
December 8	Concert

Once you have completed your broad objective outline, you must then begin to define short term goals. Realize that these lesson plans will need to be revised on a daily basis. Alterations occur because you are constantly evaluating and monitoring the progress of your band. The following daily lesson plan form has been specifically designed for the instrumental music educator.

REHEARSAL PLANNER

Date 11/20/9_

Composition	Page	Measures	Work Needed	Comments
Warm-up				
Chorale/Clark	07	all	phrasing, intonation	
			breath attacks, releases	
Chorale/Curnow	12	all	same as above	
Announcements:			a. saxophone sectional after school today	
			b. ensemble contest sign-up by Wednesday	
			c. pass out note/upcoming fundraiser	
Sinfonia 17				
Broege		Mov. II & III	II. dotted quarter acc. parts	
			II. internalize pulse/percussion	
			III. phrasing	
			III. dynamic contrast/shading	
			III. Rall. last three measures	
Allegro Brillante				
Margolis		17-21	picc. & trpt. rhythms	
		25-38	rhythm in w.w. & horns	
		58-74	art. & dynamic contrast	
		1-74	put entire section together	
An Almighty Fortress				
Shaffer		11-16	accel. & transition	
		32-38	balance/blend in brass	
			correct marc. art.	
		1-38	put entire section together	
Moorside March				
Curnow		all	sightread	
Antithigram for Band				
Stamp		4-6	meter changes in brass	
		14-37	percussion to keep pulse	
		34-36	upper w.w. runs (clean)	
		37-43	brass pyramid effect/art.	
		57-63	transition, intonation in	
			brass w/mutes	
		1-63	put entire section together	

GRADING

How does one grade in a participatory class such as band? By using a clearly defined and objective grading policy. First, find out if your school has a uniform grading scale/policy and if so, be sure to follow it. If a satisfactory/unsatisfactory or pass/fail system is in place, use it during your first year and evaluate its effectiveness. If the system is in any way impeding the progress of your students or not meeting your academic expectations, prepare a proposal of change to be implemented the succeeding year. Should no district-wide policy exist, you are responsible for designing a simple and objective grading procedure based upon personal expectations and philosophy. Remember, teachers don't give grades, students earn them. The following are examples of traditional grading scales.

Pass/Fail Grading Scale

S/P – 60 – 100%
U/F – 0 – 59%

Percentage Grading Scales

A	96-100		A	90-100
A-	90-95		B	80-89
B+	87-89		C	70-79
B	83-86		D	60-69
B-	80-82		F	0-59
C+	77-79			
C	73-76			
C-	70-72			
D+	67-69			
D	63-66			
D-	60-62			
F	0-59			

Secondly, create *primary* grading components (no more than five) to which objective and measurable criteria can be added. For example, a rehearsal grade (primary component) might include a weekly score based upon the following criteria: musical proficiencies, appropriate materials to class, attentive behavior, and attendance. The following example shows three primary components and appropriate criteria.

Rehearsal Criteria (weekly grade)

- Student on time for rehearsal
- Instrument and appropriate materials
- Attentive and exhibiting good conduct
- Attendance to all rehearsal sessions
- Performing music at a proficient level

Performance Criteria (grade for each performance)

- Student on time for performance warm-up
- Instrument and appropriate materials
- Attentive and contributing to a good performance
- Individual part performed at a high level of proficiency

Instructional Lessons (weekly grade)

- Attendance to all required lessons
- Practice goals were met (180 minutes per week)
- Lesson material performed at a high level of proficiency

Now develop a weighting system for each of your primary components. There are literally hundreds of possible weighting options, and there is no one-best-way, so carefully consider all aspects before designing this system. The following are examples of weighting options.

Rehearsals	40%
Performances	30%
Instructional Lessons	30%

Rehearsals	40%
Performances	40%
Instructional Lessons	20%

Rehearsals	50%
Performances	30%
Tests/Assignments	20%

If you have access to a computer, by all means use it to calculate grades. There are many grading programs available, and most are quite easy to learn. A computer will save you hours of time and eliminate any subjectivity on your part. Although teachers work very hard to remain objective, it is extremely difficult to neglect how influential emotions can be when evaluating learners.

In addition to the objectivity computers offer, they can average grades on short notice, calculate midsemester scores, offer statistical data such as mean scores, range, standard deviation and frequency, and can print up-to-the-minute progress reports. These reports work exceptionally well when holding parent/teacher conferences as they lend credence to your grading procedure and ensure that stated criteria is calculated without bias. The following is a sample print out.

Progress Report for Burnett, Lance

Class: Band
Quarter: 1

Current Scores (*** means missing score)
Score/Possible (Percent Score)

Score Category: Rehearsals (9 - weekly grades)
1. 88/100 2. 100/100 3. 90/100 4. 100/100 5. 90/100 6. 87/100
7. 90/100 8. 90/100 9. 100/100

Score Category: Performances (6)
1. 100/100 2. 97/100 3. 100/100 4. 80/100 5. 100/100 6. 100/100

Score Category: Instructional Lessons (9)
1. *** 2. 80/100 3. 97/100 4. 90/100 5. 95/100 6. 0/100
7. 75/100 8. 90/100 9. 86/100

Estimated Grade to Date: B

Comments

	S	U	Comments
Attendance _____			
Appropriate Materials _____			
Conduct _____			
Practice _____			
Lessons _____			
Music Learned _____			
Attitude _____			
Alert and Attentive _____			

Additional Comments:

INSTRUCTIONAL LESSONS

Have you ever wondered why some band programs are better than others? There is no full-proof masterplan that will guarantee success; however, there are two primary components that all outstanding programs possess. One, there must be exemplary teaching in the classroom and secondly, there must be a model curriculum structure in place. This curricular paradigm is known as the *dual curriculum*. The dual curriculum includes:

> Small group or individualized instruction for the development of psychomotor skill musicianship.

> Large group instruction in which to develop aesthetic sensitivity through the study and performance of exemplary music literature.

The duality of studies are of equal importance and must be taught separately and concurrently with each course of study being given sufficient time so that their unique objectives can be accomplished. Recognized authorities in the music education profession agree that without individualized instruction (instructional lessons), there is little opportunity for the development of musical skills. Without developed skills, there is insufficient opportunity for experiences with exemplary music. And, without exemplary music as the basis of instruction, there is little to justify the inclusion of instrumental music in the daily curriculum (Dean 1990, 19).

All too often instructional lessons are not considered a valid part of the curriculum, and in several states, such opportunities don't even exist. In many cases implementation of a dual curriculum would require hiring an additional director (which is not very likely), or require you to do some creative scheduling (a viable option). Ideally a lesson schedule should be individualized; however, in reality this doesn't often happen. Small group lessons should then be in homogeneous groupings by ability level. The following are examples of model instructional schedules at the middle school level.

Homogenous Groups

	M	T	W	Th.	F
(Before School)					
Time	7:30		7.30		7.30
Subject	Jazz Ens.		Jazz Ens.		Jazz Ens.
Time	8:20	8:20	8:20	8:20	8:20
Subject	8th Band	8th Band	8th Band	8th Band	8th Band
Time	9:15	9:15	9:15	9:15	9:15
Subject	A	B	C	D	E
Time	9:40	9:40	9:40	9:40	9:40
Subject	F	G	H	I	J
Time	10:10	10:10	10:10	10:10	10:10
Subject	7th Band	7th Band	7th Band	7th Band	7th Band
Time	11:05	11:05	11:05	11:05	11:05
Subject	K	L	M	N	O
Time	11:30	11:30	11:30	11:30	11:30
Subject	P	Q	R	S	T
Time	12:00	12:00	12:00	12:00	12:00
Subject	Lunch/Prep	Lunch/Prep	Lunch/Prep	Lunch/Prep	Lunch/Prep
Time	1:15	1:15	1:15	1:15	1:15
Subject	6th Band	6th Band	6th Band	6th Band	6th Band
Time	2:05	2:05	2:05	2:05	2:05
Subject	5th Band	5th Band	5th Band	5th Band	5th Band
(after school)					
Time	3:00	3:00	3:00	3:00	3:00
Subject	Make-up Lessons	Make-up Lessons	Make-up Lessons	Make-up Lessons	Make-up Lessons

A. Bruce Johnson (trpt) B. Cindy Castor (fl) C. Rene Booker (cl)
   Robert Meeks (trpt)   Greg Osteen (fl)   Scott Hanshaw (cl)
   Jill Swanson (trpt)   Heather Garside (fl)   Kyle Van Ausdall (cl)

Letters D through T also include an average of three students per lesson. Each student receives one twenty–five minute homogeneous lesson per week and a total of sixty students are serviced using this model.

Rotating Schedule – Monday

	1/5	1/12	1/19	1/26	2/2
(Before School)					
Time	7:30	7:30	7.30	7:30	7.30
Subject	Jazz Ens.	Jazz Ens.	Jazz Ens.	Jazz Ens.	Jazz Ens.
Time	8:20	8:20	8:20	8:20	8:20
Subject	8th Band	8th Band	8th Band	8th Band	8th Band
Time	9:15	9:15	9:15	9:15	9:15
Subject	A	B	C	D	E
Time	9:40	9:40	9:40	9:40	9:40
Subject	B	C	D	E	A
Time	10:10	10:10	10:10	10:10	10:10
Subject	7th Band	7th Band	7th Band	7th Band	7th Band
Time	11:05	11:05	11:05	11:05	11:05
Subject	C	D	E	A	B
Time	11:30	11:30	11:30	11:30	11:30
Subject	D	E	A	B	C
Time	12:00	12:00	12:00	12:00	12:00
Subject	Lunch/Prep	Lunch/Prep	Lunch/Prep	Lunch/Prep	Lunch/Prep
Time	1:15	1:15	1:15	1:15	1:15
Subject	6th Band	6th Band	6th Band	6th Band	6th Band
Time	2:05	2:05	2:05	2:05	2:05
Subject	5th Band	5th Band	5th Band	5th Band	5th Band
(after school)					
Time	3:00	3:00	3:00	3:00	3:00
Subject	E	A	B	C	D

A. Bruce Johnson (trpt)   B. Cindy Castor (fl)   C. Rene Booker (cl)
    Robert Meeks (trpt)   Greg Osteen (fl)   Scott Hanshaw (cl)
    Jill Swanson (trpt)   Heather Garside (fl)   Kyle Van Ausdall (cl)

Rotating Schedule – Tuesday

	1/6	1/13	1/20	1/27	2/3
(Before School) Time Subject					
Time Subject	8:20 8th Band	8:20 8th Band	8:20 8th Band	8:20 8th Band	8:20 8th Band
Time Subject	9:15 F	9:15 G	9:15 H	9:15 I	9:15 J
Time Subject	9:40 G	9:40 H	9:40 I	9:40 J	9:40 F
Time Subject	10:10 7th Band	10:10 7th Band	10:10 7th Band	10:10 7th Band	10:10 7th Band
Time Subject	11:05 H	11:05 I	11:05 J	11:05 F	11:05 G
Time Subject	11:30 I	11:30 J	11:30 F	11:30 G	11:30 H
Time Subject	12:00 Lunch/Prep	12:00 Lunch/Prep	12:00 Lunch/Prep	12:00 Lunch/Prep	12:00 Lunch/Prep
Time Subject	1:15 6th Band	1:15 6th Band	1:15 6th Band	1:15 6th Band	1:15 6th Band
Time Subject	2:05 5th Band	2:05 5th Band	2:05 5th Band	2:05 5th Band	2:05 5th Band
(after school) Time Subject	3:00 J	3:00 F	3:00 G	3:00 H	3:00 I

F. Diana Sims (tuba)
   Glen Harrod (tuba)
   Eric Gruber (tuba)

G. Dan Cudworth (trb)
   Janet Hindman (trb)
   Robert Lundien (trb)

H. Dyan Hamp (cl)
   Sue Leyda (cl)
   Mel Baker (cl)

The rotating schedule allows each student's lesson to remain on the same day; however, the time alternates.

Six – Day Cycle

	Day 1	Day 2	Day 3	Day 4	Day 5	Day 6
(Before School)						
Time	7:30		7.30		7.30	
Subject	Jazz Ens.		Jazz Ens.		Jazz Ens.	
Time	8:20	8:20	8:20	8:20	8:20	8:20
Subject	8th Band	8th Band	8th Band	8th Band	8th Band	8th Band
Time	9:15	9:15	9:15	9:15	9:15	9:15
Subject	A	B	C	D	E	F
Time	9:40	9:40	9:40	9:40	9:40	9:40
Subject	G	H	I	J	K	L
Time	10:10	10:10	10:10	10:10	10:10	10:10
Subject	7th Band	7th Band	7th Band	7th Band	7th Band	7th Band
Time	11:05	11:05	11:05	11:05	11:05	11:05
Subject	M	N	O	P	Q	R
Time	11:30	11:30	11:30	11:30	11:30	11:30
Subject	S	T	U	V	W	X
Time	12:00	12:00	12:00	12:00	12:00	12:00
Subject	Lunch/Prep	Lunch/Prep	Lunch/Prep	Lunch/Prep	Lunch/Prep	Lunch/Prep
Time	1:15	1:15	1:15	1:15	1:15	1:15
Subject	6th Band	6th Band	6th Band	6th Band	6th Band	6th Band
Time	2:05	2:05	2:05	2:05	2:05	2:05
Subject	5th Band	5th Band	5th Band	5th Band	5th Band	5th Band
(after school)						
Time	3:00	3:00	3:00	3:00	3:00	3:00
Subject	Make-up Lessons	Make-up Lessons	Make-up Lessons	Make-up Lessons	Make-up Lessons	Make-up Lessons

A. Bruce Johnson (trpt)　　B. Cindy Castor (fl)　　C. Rene Booker (cl)
   Robert Meeks (trpt)　　　　Greg Osteen (fl)　　　　Scott Hanshaw (cl)
   Jill Swanson (trpt)　　　　 Heather Garside (fl)　　 Kyle Van Ausdall (cl)

This schedule permits twenty–four lesson slots at twenty–five minutes per student every sixth day. At an average of three students per slot one can accommodate seventy–two students.

There are many scheduling models currently in place, and be assured that more will follow. School systems seem more than willing to implement the next *sure-proof* schedule that promises to solve the educational and social woes of the day. Modular, block, floating, six–day cycles, and eight period days are only a few examples of a system inundated with scheduling alternatives. Learn the school's scheduling process and then use it to your educational advantage.

If you enter a situation where no instructional lesson schedule exists, prepare a proposal of change for the following year. Your request must be developed with great care, as administrators will evaluate all aspects of your plan. The following items should be considered when preparing your presentation.

Put your proposal in writing. This should be a short overview of the lesson proposal with rationale for acceptance. Include the philosophy behind the dual curriculum.

Creative scheduling is your best chance to implement or enhance an instructional lesson schedule. Be open to altering your schedule in order to make room for lessons. For example, if you have a seventh grade band rehearsal every day, would you be willing to schedule three rehearsals per week using the other two time slots for instructional lessons? Would it be possible and would you be willing to schedule lessons before and after school as well as during your preparation period? Would your administrator be willing to allow students to leave a study hall or class to attend a lesson? The old adage *where there is a will there is a way* readily applies.

Talk with other directors. Research area schools to find out where similar lesson schedules are established. These directors can help you prepare your written and verbal presentations and give you insight into objections you might face.

Go for broke. Propose a schedule in which each child would receive one thirty minute homogeneous small group (2-4) lesson per week. Make an exciting and positive presentation explaining that your proposal is a proven curricular practice.

Don't spread the news. Work directly through your immediate supervisor and sell them on the curricular addition/alteration. Teachers from other disciplines may have a host of biased reasons why your plan will not work.

Schedule a follow-up meeting. Schedule this meeting within two weeks of your presentation date. A time frame any longer than this and your proposal will most likely be buried in a pile on your supervisor's desk – not in neglect, but only because the crisis of the day takes precedence. Offer to hold the follow–up meeting before school, during lunch, after school, or during an evening if need be.

Be flexible and creative. If your original proposal is not accepted, find out what changes would make it workable. Allow your administrator to have ownership in the project. By posing questions such as, "Would this possibly work?" and "How do you feel about this?" you welcome their involvement.

Make it work! Whatever plan is agreed upon, *make it work*! If you proposed a weekly thirty minute group lesson and your administrator, as a final suggestion, offers one fifteen minute group lesson every other week, take it and run! This is a definite curricular improvement and you can always make future proposals.

Once your schedule is in place, use specific lesson material with your students. *Don't use band music in a lesson situation*! The entire concept of the dual curriculum is based upon the belief that this mode of instruction is equal but separate; the lesson itself must have goals and objectives different from the large ensemble. It is simply not sound educational philosophy to use this small group setting to *re-rehearse* large group music.

After sending your administrator a thank–you note for their role in making the lesson schedule a reality, make a personal visit three or four weeks later to report the musical growth you have witnessed. Also relay any parental compliments and notes of appreciation regarding the lesson addition/alteration. With the schedule in place, you now have a curricular structure that, coupled with exemplary teaching, will allow you to see marked musical growth in your students and ensembles. If you are unable to persuade your administrator to implement the instructional lesson schedule, private lessons are a viable option.

PRIVATE INSTRUCTION

Imagine the performance level of your band if every student studied with a private teacher. Although it is unrealistic to expect one hundred percent participation, it is a worthwhile pursuit. Better band programs almost always have a large percentage of students studying privately and numerous mediocre programs have been turned around in a few short years by promoting this tutelage.

If your program has no one studying privately, the following four steps will help you set sail. Your first assignment is to locate and speak with potential private teachers. Most likely these will be people within the community or surrounding area who have teaching experience. Make sure you feel comfortable in recommending these individuals. Secondly, prepare a list of private teachers (to be passed out) and make an exciting announcement during band rehearsal encouraging private study. Thirdly, mail a letter to parents calling their attention to this educational opportunity. Most parents are very open to offering their child private lessons; they simply need assistance with the process. A draft letter is shown in the following example.

Royal Heights Middle School Band

Mr. Bradley A. Johnson

October 1, 199_

Dear Parent(s)/Guardian(s):

Greetings! Just a short note to let you know how much I enjoy having your child in band this year. We are off to a running start and busy preparing to march the annual Maple Leaf Parade in LeMars next Saturday.

I would like to encourage you to offer your child the opportunity to take private lessons outside of school. Research shows that students who study privately succeed at a higher level and progress more rapidly. In addition, it makes playing an instrument more enjoyable. Below is a list of qualified area teachers who currently have openings.

Feel free to contact me at school if you have questions.

Sincerely,

Bradley A. Johnson
Director of Bands

LIST OF RECOMMENDED PRIVATE TEACHERS

Jeff Taylor	Jerry Schultz	Amy Yoder
1320 North E. St.	801 South Davis St.	35 6th Avenue N.E.
Joplin, MO 64801	Webb City, MO 64722	Joplin, MO 64801
417-625-6748	417-623-8001	417-625-7590
(brass & percussion)	(brass & percussion)	(all instruments)
William Lester	Joanie Martin	Shandrika Dozier
345 Lynwood Avenue	10 Friendly Lane	552 Leighton
Joplin, MO 64801	Carlsburg, MO 64709	Joplin, MO 64801
417-625-6638	417-626-3445	417-625-7112
(woodwinds)	(woodwinds)	(all instruments)

A week following the mailing, canvas your students to see if they have seriously sought private instruction. If not, encourage them to visit with their parents about this. As a final service, phone those parents whose children have obvious potential or exceptional talent, and encourage them to consider this opportunity. An introductory line might include ". . . Greg certainly has a lot of musical talent and I know he would benefit from taking lessons with a private instructor. Have you given this any consideration?" Once you have completed these four steps, yield to the parents and allow them to make contact with the teacher. If the results of this designed effort are not what you anticipated, repeat the process at mid-year and/or promote private instruction during parent/teacher conferences.

If you are located in a remote area or small town and don't have access to a corp of private teachers, consider starting your own studio. This is an excellent way of offering a service to students and parents, and you can earn additional money to pay off those ensuing school loans. Private lesson fees vary depending upon your geographical location, so check surrounding areas for current rates. If you are promoting yourself as an instructor, a verbal statement followed by a note sent home to parents will suffice. Your promotion should be a bit more subdued because an intense approach may lead some parents to believe you are using your teaching position as a mechanism for financial gain.

STUDENT PRACTICE

Students must know your expectations with regard to individual practice. An excellent way of encouraging this self–discipline is the use of a band award system and/or practice card. Practice is often tedious, and the word itself has a negative connotation; therefore, you may wish to refer to this card as a *record of achievement*. Most directors strongly encourage one hundred eighty minutes of practice per week and use this as part of the grading criteria. Once a student enters high school, formal documentation is not needed, for personal responsibility comes into play. Practice cards are often printed in method books; however, many directors prefer to design their own. The following is a sample record of achievement.

RECORD OF ACHIEVEMENT

Sunday	Monday	Tuesday	Wednesday	Thursday	Friday	Saturday

There are a number of outstanding band award systems on the market and many directors find this type of positive reinforcement to be most productive. Select the system that meets your standards and matches your philosophy of monitoring and rewarding students. You can also enhance practice sessions by requiring young students to purchase the tapes or CDs which accompany beginning method books. Recorded solo accompaniments are also available at the secondary level. Most major publishing companies (listed in appendix) offer these accompaniment series which not only make practice more enjoyable, but teach a host of musical skills.

Another effective way of encouraging practice is to involve parents in the process. Send a letter to all elementary and middle school/junior high band parents listing ways in which they can enhance their child's practice sessions. The following communication is a blueprint.

Royal Heights Elementary Band   Mr. Bradley A. Johnson
                                                           Director of Bands

September 3, 199_

Dear Parent(s)/Guardian(s):

Greetings from the Royal Heights Band Department! This year has started off in great fashion as our first rehearsal was a tremendous success. We were able to sightread three pieces. I look forward to more outstanding rehearsals.

Individual student practice is most important for the continued musical growth of your child. I strongly encourage thirty minutes of daily practice (180 minutes per week) on assigned lesson material. You can help your child meet this practice goal when you:

- **Plan a scheduled time each day for practice**

- **Select a time after school when your child has the most energy**

- Find a quiet place away from any disturbances

- Help set a goal for each practice session

- Provide a straight–backed chair and music stand

- Sit with your budding musician as they practice

- Praise your child for their efforts and progress

Please note that your child will be asking you to initial their *RECORD OF ACHIEVEMENT* prior to their weekly lesson. If you have any questions regarding practice procedures, feel free to contact me at school. Thank you for your help in this matter.

Sincerely,

Bradley A. Johnson
Director of Bands

AUDITIONS & CHAIR PLACEMENT

Although there is debate over philosophy and methodology, the fact remains that most directors advocate some form of standardized audition and placement procedure. Obviously an individual audition must take place in order for you to evaluate the strengths and weaknesses of your personnel. Hearing each student will assist you in selecting the proper level of literature and setting realistic goals. Begin by developing objective criteria for the audition (i.e. articulation, phrasing, scales, tone, sightreading, etc.).

Because elaborate scoring formulas consume time and energy, create a tabulation system that is simple and straightforward. Leave a portion of the audition open–ended. For example, afford students the opportunity to perform additional scales beyond the required amount, or allow them to include a prepared etude or solo excerpt. Students equate this empowerment with fairness. Inform them in advance of all audition requirements and scoring criteria by posting the adjudication form. There should be no mysteries in this process.

The following are examples of audition requirements.

ROYAL HEIGHTS HIGH SCHOOL BAND
AUDITION REQUIREMENTS

TROMBONES & EUPHONIUMS

Major scales: 5 sharps - 5 flats, chromatic (@ 120)
Etudes: *Melodious Etudes for Trombone* by Joannes Rochut: page 10, #9; page 17, #15
Prepared etude or solo excerpt: student choice
Sightreading:

CLARINETS

Major scales: 5 sharps - 5 flats, chromatic (@ 120)
Etudes: *Selected Studies* by Himie Voxman: page 4 and page 9
Prepared etude or solo excerpt: student choice
Sightreading:

BAND AUDITION FORM

NAME   Nathan Camp   INSTRUMENT   Trombone

60 Points Possible	Comments	Score
Scales (10)		8.5
Tone (10)	*good low register*	8.5
Articulation (10)	*legato articulation needs attention*	6.5
Musicality/Phrasing (10)		7.5
Sightreading (if applicable) Etude/Solo (10)		8
Rhythm (10)	*strong*	8

TOTAL___47___

Comments: *May have difficult time with higher (1st part) range.*
            Solid player.

In most cases, you will be the only person auditioning your students; however, if there is another director available, include them as an additional source. Once you have completed the tabulations, chart each section by score. This information can then be made available to students who desire to discern their score.

TROMBONES

Score	Name
58	Trevor Headrick
50	Lynn McDonald
47	Nathan Camp
46	Rob Lundien
42	Abel Stewart
40	Karen Cameron
39	Robert Vice
31	Carlene Boyer

To avoid embarrassing your students when announcing audition results, simply post a diagram depicting the seating arrangement. Upon entering the room, students will locate their placement and take their seats. This prevents calling out names in the order of scores, and the diagram can then be used as a seating chart.

There are many options when seating and arranging your musicians on parts. The following three are frequently used.

Seating by audition points; beginning with first chair and moving continuously through the entire section.

Seating by audition points; in the following order; first chair, first part – first chair, second part – first chair, third part – second chair, first part – second chair, second part, etc.

Alternate parts on a rotating basis; directors who use a rotational configuration have students alternate parts and chairs on different musical selections.

It is also possible to use variations or combinations of the above. Each of these seating arrangements has advantages and disadvantages, so consider all of your options and implement the arrangement that will work best in your situation.

CHALLENGES

Implementing a challenge system places a premium on chair and part placement. The system can be likened to a play-off, with the winner acquiring the superior seat. This offers students the opportunity to challenge the individual seated in the chair ahead of them in an attempt to advance in the section. For example, if your second chair flutist challenges the first chair player and prevails, they exchange seats. The new principal player is then considered the section leader and is afforded any solo opportunities that accompany first chair.

When properly administered, this system is a solvent motivator because it offers a worthwhile goal. Challenge systems, with all of their variations, have been successfully used for many years and are a proven and credible way to enhance student skills. It is not recommended that this be promoted at the elementary level as students are not mature enough to handle this type of competition. Be aware that parents may not understand the philosophy behind this practice, especially if you are presenting it as a new concept. If you implement a challenge policy, be sure to include the guidelines in your band handbook. The following is an example of challenge procedures and criteria.

CHALLENGE ADJUDICATION FORM

DATE   10/17/9_   INSTRUMENT   Clarinet

60 Points Possible	Comments	#1	#2
Scales (10)		7.5	8
Tone (10)		6	7
Articulation (10)		9	8
Musicality/Phrasing (10)		7	5.5
Sightreading (if applicable) Etude/Solo (10)		6	6
Rhythm (10)		8	7
	TOTAL	* 43.5	41.5

Comments:
  Both performed well. Musicality/phrasing made the difference.
  #1 performed with more musical expression and dynamic contrast.

CHALLENGE GUIDELINES

1. Each student will be allowed to challenge a maximum of three times per semester.
2. You may challenge only the person seated directly ahead of you.
3. Any challenge that is refused is lost (some students may prefer not to take part and are therefore not required to accept the challenge).
4. Challenge music is selected by the director and is given to the students one week prior to the challenge date. Selections might include etude excerpts, scales, sections from band music, and sightreading.
5. All challenges are taped in a practice room on cassette recorder. This provides anonymity and objective adjudication.
6. Results will be posted within two (2) school days.
7. Adjudication challenge criteria is seen in the previous form.

BUDGET

When you inherit a band program, you also inherit the district budget structure. Unfortunately, many public and parochial schools do not have the financial means to properly maintain an adequate budget. Some districts choose to funnel monies to other areas, and almost all schools have at one time or another placed the arts on the proverbial chopping block. Most districts begin financial planning six to eight months prior to the upcoming school year, so your request for additional funding must be documented well in advance. The following is an example of what a district budgetary request might look like.

TO: Thomas E. Davis
FROM: Bradley A. Johnson *(your initials)*
DATE: December 12, 199_
RE: 199_ – 9_ Budget Requests

The following 199_ – 9_ budget request has been researched and
the music company with the lowest bid is listed.

INSTRUCTIONAL SUPPLIES

Music
a. marching, concert, jazz, small ensemble   400.00 Wingert-Jones Music

Books
a. group warm-up books   45.00 Wingert-Jones Music

Recording Materials
a. blank cassette tapes   22.50 Wal-Mart

Miscellaneous
a. manuscript paper   16.00 Williamson Music

SUBTOTAL 483.50

EQUIPMENT

Instruments
a. Euphonium (model 422-Y)   848.00 Sorden Music
b. Snare Drum (model 20-L)   230.00 Ray's Mid-Bell Music
c. Tuba (H-779)   3,240.00 Ray's Mid-Bell Music

Repair
a. Tenor Saxophone - check & adjust   48.00 West Music
b. Tuba - flush   46.00 West Music
c. Bass Clarinet - check & adjust   39.00 West Music
d. Baritone Saxophone - check & adjust   75.00 West Music
e. Drum Heads   130.00 Sorden Music
f. Miscellaneous Repair   500.00
g. Miscellaneous Equipment   500.00

SUBTOTAL   5,656.00

SPECIAL PROJECTS

a. Travel   270.00   District Buses
b. Programs   140.00   Red's Printing

               SUBTOTAL   410.00

        TOTAL BUDGET REQUEST   6,549.50

PART FOUR

RELATIONSHIPS

Knowledge is the treasure, but judgment the treasurer of a wise man.

– William Penn

THE KEYMAKERS

Some people see a closed door and turn away. Others see a closed door, try the knob, if it doesn't open . . . they turn away. Still others see a closed door, try the knob, if it doesn't open, they find a key, if the key doesn't fit . . . they turn away. A rare few see a closed door, try the knob, if it doesn't open, they find a key, if the key doesn't fit . . . they make one.

COMMUNICATION

On the surface, a section on *relationships* may seem out of place in a book focussing on band directing; however, good relationships begin with skillful communication: the most valuable of all professional traits. The often quoted saying; a gossip talks about others, a bore talks about himself/herself, and a brilliant conversationalist talks about you, is inherently true. Coming into your own as a communicator is largely a *personal growth* process which includes the following four steps.

Self-Awareness. Good communication skills begin with a positive self-image. This is a matter of getting in touch with who you are at any given moment in a relationship, being aware of your own self in relation to the person you are communicating with.

Self-Assessment. Self-assessment is a keen awareness of the self and then some, in that it involves a diagnostic evaluation of your communicative strengths and weaknesses. If communication is a weakness, take a verbal skills class, enroll in a video course, or read a self-help book to enhance your shortcomings.

Self-Direction. You must be a self–starter who can determine the course of personal destiny through communication. Refuse to allow yourself to be defeated by external circumstances.

Self-Actualization. This is the goal, the end result which you strive to accomplish. Have you become the communicator you want to be?

Your first task as a communicator is to determine how you will handle comments and questions regarding your predecessor. Realize that you are entering a situation in which a prior relationship exists between your new students and their former teacher. When situations or conversations arise regarding the previous director, be willing to compliment your colleague, then steer the conversation to the present. Never state a negative about a predecessor, for there is nothing to be gained through this type of criticism.

TAMING DRAGONS

With the unprecedented changes occurring in public schools, and society placing unrealistic demands upon the educational system, educators have more than their fair share of relational conflict. Working with administrators, students, colleagues, and parents often produces a relational tug–of–war in an already tumultuous environment.

Managing conflict in a positive manner is a precious commodity, but learning how to *preclude* conflict is a professional necessity. Relational conflict occurs because others are not like us. The educational kettle contains myriads of people with various backgrounds, perspectives, ability levels, and interests. The only way to keep conflict from ever occurring is to control all of the people and events in your life – an obvious impossibility! The difference between success and failure during your first year is often the knowledge and ability to *preclude* conflict by means of communicative strategies. You cannot regulate the responses of others and entirely eliminate conflict, but you can implement some personal attitudes and behaviors that help reduce the frequency.

Confront tension early. Go with your intuition. If you sense tension developing, it is not a figment of your imagination; others are sensing it as well. At this point, no one has been hurt and no personal and irrevocable animosities have developed. This is the best time to simply say, "I think we need some clarification" and confront the issue at hand. Confrontation may be difficult for those whose personality favors avoidance, and although playing ostrich allows you to bury your head, it also exposes other vulnerable body parts.

Attack problems – not people. Approach obstacles as issues to be solved, rather than enemies to be defeated. When opinions are attacked and characters maligned, personal resentments act as a major obstacle to reaching solutions. By attacking issues instead of people, threats are reduced, and destructive conflict can be precluded. Keep the common goal in mind: educating students.

Do what you expect of others. If you expect others to be kind, considerate, honest, open, and true to their word, then you must do likewise. Have you noticed that we rarely hold ourselves accountable to the same standard that we demand of others? Living by the Golden Rule will go a long way in precluding relational conflict. Setting a positive example is one of the best ways of influencing others, for character is based more on what we *do* than what we *say*.

Practice self-examination. Realize that you are not always right, your methods are not always the best, and others have valid ideas. Remarks such as "I never thought of it in that light," or "that seems to be a better idea," signal that you are open and willing to examine even your own sacred cows. Introspection enhances a learning and growing attitude.

Choose your issues carefully. Not everything is worth dying for. Focus on your priorities and allow lesser issues to fall by the wayside. Sharpening the battle–ax over every concern consumes your energies and is emotionally draining. Keep the big picture in mind, stay tuned to your priorities, and be willing to lose a few battles in order to win the war.

Communication begins with listening, not talking. Once others feel understood, they will be more open to your ideas. Merely waiting to respond while your mind races to formulate a reply does not constitute listening. Listening is an art form and involves hearing both the content and feelings of the speaker. Because good listening skills are usually not taught or modeled, they will take practice and effort.

Feedback helps clarify misunderstanding. To find out if you are being understood or are understanding others, simply ask. Statements such as, "So what you're saying is . . ." and "If I understand you correctly . . ." let you know whether or not comprehension has occurred. Observe nonverbal signals as well: hesitations, bewildered looks, rolling eyes, aloofness, or fidgeting provide clues to solving the puzzle of understanding.

Build the trust factor. When trust is high, conflict is low. Five ingredients make up trust: affirmation, acceptance, support, integrity, and respect. It is often the seemingly small things that build trust, such as keeping your word, remembering to introduce a guest, telling someone how much their presence means to you, and acknowledging the contributions of administrators, colleagues, parents, and students.

People tend to support what they help to create. Disregard the ideas and opinions of others, and conflict will inevitably strike. For example, seeking advice from your administration when developing a classroom policy or procedure (band handbook) affords them input and ownership toward the final product.

There will always be antagonists. It doesn't matter where you are or what you do, well–intentioned, and not–so–well–intentioned dragons will appear. Their names and faces change, but the destruction they cause remains the same. **You cannot slay dragons, but you can tame them**.

This article appeared in slightly different form in *Learning* magazine and was authored by Phillip C. Wise and Terry S. Wise. Reprinted by permission from the September/October 1996 issue of *Learning* TM, Copyright The Education Center, Inc.

ADMINISTRATION

Maintain and nurture these relationships, for these individuals are an invaluable asset. In truth, your building principal can be your best friend and strongest advocate. By following the chain of command and all building and district procedures, you will quickly strengthen this alliance. If you are unclear as to proceedings, ask for clarification or guidance. If you wish to propose change, proceed judiciously through proper channels, as educators who break protocol do not succeed in the long run. Until the change occurs, follow all school policies – *don't buck the system*. The following are relational guidelines when working with administration.

Keep your administrator informed. Your administrator should be kept abreast of happenings in your department. It is not necessary to inform your principal of everything you do, but keep him/her apprised of more important issues.

Be professional. Reread this section in Part Two.

Be patient. Some directors mistakenly believe that all administrators have backgrounds in the *perspiring arts* and won't support music, under any circumstance. It is true that many administrators have athletic backgrounds and view the arts from a different perspective; however, this doesn't mean they will not be supportive. Although part of their job description is to promote faculty and programs, administrators wear numerous hats and struggle to find the time to endorse and assist to the degree that is sometimes expected.

Present solutions, not problems. Your administrator will appreciate a positive attitude and solutions to your concerns. Consider your principal to be a sounding–board, not a dumping–ground. If you approach your principal with a problem, be sure to offer a solution.

Education = understanding. Should you discover that your principal has little understanding of music education, you may wish to embark upon an educational tutelage. This must be done with great care so as not to intimidate or supersede their authority. Begin by sending copies of journal articles that highlight the educational value of music. Submitting an article every few months will show that you are an avid reader (which you should be) and are working to better the school's music program. There are many exceptional sources from which to extract materials (professional journal listing in appendix).

COLLEAGUES

Educators share a common goal: their sincere love for teaching children. As you assume your new role, look for a friend or mentor within faculty circles. This person can be invaluable as you venture through the inaugural year. Professionalism includes the ability to work *collaboratively* with your colleagues. Be enthusiastic and proactive in your approach rather than subservient and reactive. True collegial respect evolves from behaving and responding in a professional manner.

Some of your colleagues will not appreciate music to the same extent that you do. Others may label it a trivial extra curricular activity. Your relational objective is to treat these coworkers with respect, while being mindful that not all will befriend you or your program. All jobs in the education field are difficult, so acknowledge the importance of your colleagues, regardless of their views toward music.

Professional jealousy is another relational situation you may encounter, especially if you make a positive impression on your administration and students during the first few months of school. Jealousy occurs for many reasons: a successful program, awards, honors, and personality conflicts to name a few. Although this form of mistrust is the exception rather than the rule, you must not be caught off guard by these individuals who feel threatened or insecure. There will always be antagonists who have locked their doors of optimism and thrown away the key. Remain professional and continue to be respectful to these foreboding individuals, while not going out of your way to make contact.

Maintenance Personnel

The custodial staff should be on your top ten list of best friends. Over the course of your first year, you will need assistance with setting–up, tearing-down, moving equipment, and a host of other items that will inevitably pop up. Support from the maintenance staff can also be beneficial when additional music cabinets or storage shelves need to be built. Befriend this hardworking crew and treat them with great respect as they do an invaluable job that is often overlooked.

If you find your custodial staff enjoys coconut cream pie or chocolate chip cookies, purchase some *goodies* for them in recognition of their hard work. A few kind words and a small token of appreciation to these important people will make your job much easier. Once a task has been completed for you, you know what to do: send a thank–you note.

School Board

In most cases you will seldom fraternize with the district school board; however, when the occasion arises, be open and friendly. Treat board members with deference as they have volunteered their time to assist with the educational process. The majority of these officials are well–intentioned in their undertaking of responsibilities and are pleased when high standards of achievement are attained. District boards tend to focus on three primary areas when evaluating school music programs.

• The production of musical achievements

• The adherence and enforcement of school policy

• Parental and community support of the program

Secure the names and addresses of each board member and send them invitations to your performances. You should also inform them of any community service the band is involved with. The following is a letter of invitation which serves as a model.

Royal Heights High School Band   *Bradley A. Johnson*

May 8, 199_

Mrs. Eva Eslinger
Board Member, Royal Heights Public School District
133 Oakdale Avenue
Royal Heights, MO 64801

Dear Mrs. Eslinger:

I trust this letter finds you in good health and enjoying the beginnings of a beautiful spring. The band has welcomed the opportunity to be outside in preparation for the annual Tulip Festival Parade which takes place in Pella on May 29th.

I wish to personally invite you to attend our final concert band performance Monday, May 14, at 7:30 p.m. in the high school auditorium. This promises to be an exciting evening as we will be performing a theme concert featuring a patriotic salute to America. In addition, we will be presenting student music awards.

Last Thursday evening our brass choir had the good fortune of performing for the Leighton Leisure Living Senior Center. The audience enjoyed the music and was very appreciative. We have accepted an invitation to return next fall.

If your schedule will allow, I know you will enjoy this evening of music.

Sincerely yours,

Bradley A. Johnson
Director of Bands

COMMUNITY

It will not take long to locate the movers and shakers of the community. These people have the ability to assist you with your program needs. For example, if you know that one of your student's parents was a former music teacher, make an effort to contact this fellow musician. Chances are you have found a supporter. Perhaps a local businessperson is a music advocate. If so, patronize his/her store (if possible) and get acquainted. Nurture these kinds of relationships with the prospect that these new friends will serve as leaders when you begin raising money to procure band uniforms or some other large scale purchase. Be creative and use all of your personal and relational savvy when dealing with the community. The following is a checklist which offers innovative ways to open the doors of support.

- Write a letter to the editor (local newspaper) thanking the community for attending a band concert.

- Send complimentary music event tickets to community leaders.

- Make a presentation about the band program to civic leaders or business organizations (Rotary, Lions, etc.).

- Prepare a fact sheet about the band program and mail to community advocates.

- Create a promotional video of the band program to enhance public awareness.

- Solicit community feedback.

- Collaborate with a community task force to build support.

- Publicize *Music In Our Schools Month* and encourage participation.

- Join or serve on a committee (Library, United Way, Arts Council, etc.).

- Mail personal concert invitations to city leaders and advocates.

- Propose that the district provide bus transportation for area nursing home/senior housing residents so they may attend a concert.

BOOSTER ORGANIZATION

Booster organizations can be invaluable to your program; however, this unique relationship places you in the middle of many people: students, parents, administration, and community. This can be a precarious situation if you are not organized and *prepared to lead.*

Of primary consideration is the structure upon which the organization is based. Your first order of business is to read the institutional bylaws and determine the philosophy for which the organization was established. If none exist, it is in your best interest, and the interest of the order, to propose this be done. Request bylaws from area booster groups or furnish the association with the following model outline.

Royal Heights Band Boosters
199_ – 9_ Organizational Bylaws

ARTICLE I – NAME

The name of this organization shall be called the *Royal Heights Band Boosters.*

ARTICLE II – OBJECTIVE

This organizat on was established to promote the general welfare of the band by supporting the district, school, and music department philosophies and policies. This organization serves as a *supportive* group working to enhance and labor with the district, school, and band director(s).

ARTICLE III – MEMBERSHIP AND DUES

Section 1: Parent(s)/Guardian(s) of all band students are considered members of the organization.
Section 2: There shall be no membership dues for the 199_ – 9_ school year.

ARTICLE IV – MEETINGS

Section 1: Regular meetings shall be held on the first Tuesday of each month at 7:30 p.m. in the bandroom unless other–wise designated.

ARTICLE V – OFFICERS AND ELECTIONS

Section 1: Officers shall be President, Vice-President, Secretary, and Treasurer.
Section 2: These officers shall be elected at the April meeting. Officers shall serve for a term of one year. No one may hold the same office for more than two consecutive years.
Section 3: Nominations shall be made by a nominating committee appointed by the President one month prior to the election of officers. They shall present at the election meeting the names of at least one candidate for each office to be filled. The consent of each candidate must be obtained before his/her name may be placed in nomination. Additional nominations may be made from the floor.

Section 4: A vacancy occurring in an office shall be filled by a vote from the members of this organization following nominations from the floor.

Section 5: Officers will be installed at the May meeting.

ARTICLE VI – DUTIES OF THE OFFICERS

Section 1: The President shall preside at all meetings of both the general organization and of the executive board and shall perform all other duties usually pertaining to that office. The President's name shall appear on the savings and checking accounts of this organization. The President will only withdraw monies from accounts in the event the treasurer is unavailable and bills must be paid before the treasurer will be able to do so.

Section 2: The Vice-President shall preside in the absence of the President, assist the President and other officers, and act as historian. At no less than one meeting during the year the Vice-President will read the bylaws to see if any revisions are proposed.

Section 3: The Secretary shall keep a correct record of the proceedings of all meetings, act as press correspondent, and shall perform such other duties as may be delegated to him/her.

Section 4: The Treasurer shall receive all monies of the organization and keep an accurate record of receipts and expenditures, and in addition, shall be responsible for presenting all year-end records to the school district's business manager for review and audit.

ARTICLE VII – STANDING COMMITTEES

Section 1: The executive board shall consist of the elective officers of the band boosters, and the band director(s).

ARTICLE VIII – EQUIPMENT

Section 1: Any instrument or equipment purchased entirely, or in part by the boosters shall be primarily for the Royal Heights Band Program.

Section 2: An official list of instruments and equipment purchased by the band boosters shall be kept by the Secretary and band director(s). Additional copies shall be kept in the school office and district business office.

Section 3: Before uniforms, instruments, or equipment are purchased with booster money, the organization must receive a written bid to be voted upon. Such purchases must be approved by a simple majority of the members present.

ARTICLE IX – AMENDMENTS

These bylaws may be amended at any regular meeting of the organization by a two–thirds (2/3) vote of the members present, providing the membership was given notice of the intended vote at the previous meeting.

ARTICLE X – RULES OF ORDER

This organization shall be governed by *Robert's Rules of Order* unless they conflict with these bylaws.

Originally submitted (date)
(* List names of executive board members)

Revised on (date)
(* List names of executive board members)

Each booster meeting should have an itinerary. If one doesn't exist and meetings are run *off–the–cuff* (usually counterproductive), work with your booster president to establish an agenda. This will allow for an organized and more productive meeting. The following is an itinerary example.

Royal Heights Band Booster Meeting

April 7, 199_

Meeting to Order:
> Special Music – Clarinet Trio (Liliana Valencia, Amy
> Steinkuehler, Keith Talley)

Minutes of Past Meeting

Financial Report

Old Business:
> Solo/Ensemble Contest Concessions Report

New Business:
> Spring Reception
> Summer Music Camp Scholarships

Other Business

Meeting Conclusion

Establish the fact that your booster group is a consortium designed to *enhance* the program, not *run* the program. If there is one downfall to this type of association, it is that they tend to misunderstand their charge. Some members believe they are entitled to schedule performances, select music, and make program decisions that enter into your professional domain. Empower your booster group to be active by enlisting their help in established projects while at the same time *channeling their efforts.* These activities may include fundraising duties, planning special events, concert promotion, and community contacts. In a very delicate, yet firm and professional manner, convert their charge into policy supporter. *Lead them gently or they will lead you.*

Share accomplishments and upcoming events with your booster group. However, it is not in your best interest to present long–term goals that are under consideration. For example, if you are contemplating a band trip to Florida in two years, it is not wise to make a public statement without first establishing the proper groundwork (i.e. contacting administration, estimating expenses, etc.). A premature announcement can only be a hindrance.

As with all established institutions, traditionalism sometimes impedes contemporary thought. If you inherit a booster group that is leading the program, *move slowly*. Follow the determined path – in this case the path of least resistance – and carefully observe the workings. Find out the identity of the *players,* the *dynamics* of the group, and the *ways of the land* (this middle–of–the–road approach is outlined in Part One). Any attempt to immediately alter such a self–empowered enclave could result in your demise, for booster groups can be a make or break situation. Establish a solid working relationship with all members of the executive board, while seeking advocates who are supportive of your ideology.

PARENT TEACHER CONFERENCES

Parent/Teacher conferences can be a strenuous time for the first year educator. Parents also enter this arena with mixed emotions and many of the same concerns. One of the keys to a successful first conference is to establish communication; after all, you are *partners* in the child's educational experience.

The Parent/Teacher Guidepost

Hold the conference away from your desk. Placing the desk between you and the parent(s) builds an automatic barrier. An open area where you are seated face–to–face, with a table positioned at your side for student files will work well. Arrange a chair for you, two chairs for parent(s), and have additional seats available in the event the student and/or other family members attend. Individual classrooms work best, as they provide privacy and confidentiality.

Don't rush the conference. Although fifteen or twenty minute intervals are usually adequate, take the time needed to allow parents to become relaxed in the situation. If you feel the conference needs additional time, schedule a follow–up meeting.

Listen carefully. Good listening skills are invaluable. Utilizing this ability will enable you to gain insight into the parent(s) and student. Tact teaches you when to be silent and when to speak; inquirers who are always inquiring never learn anything.

Examine your emotional reaction to criticism. Some parents will view this meeting as an invitation to speak unfavorably about you or your policies. Disguise any hostility you may feel, and don't overreact to this criticism. When differences occur, remain congenial, speak softly and without animosity. Stand up for what you believe, take the highroad, and remain the consummate professional you are.

Decide in advance what will be discussed during the conference. If you are grading by computer, prepare a progress grade report for each parent. Have a personal file (form shown in appendix) on each student, and review your notes prior to the conference. Items to prepare for discussion are listed below.

- Musical progress
- Work habits
- Social adjustments and peer relationships
- Interests, aptitudes, and abilities
- Interaction with teachers and staff
- Health or emotional concerns
- Response to class rules and procedures

Speak plain English. Use the simplest and clearest words possible when explaining the student's progress. Refrain from using educational and technical jargon. By the same token, don't talk down to parents, for they will resent being treated like a child.

Don't allow comments about other students to enter into the conversation. Parents attend conferences to hear about their child, not others. It is simply not professional to discuss or compare one child to another during this meeting. In the event a parent inquires about the progress of another student, state, "I am not at liberty to discuss that with you. That is confidential information."

Provide parents with at least one action-step. This step should be a specific request to assist the child in accomplishing a structured goal. In all likelihood, you will be requesting that the majority of parents support their child's practice habits. Prepare a guide sheet to give to parents as their action–step. Other action–steps might include: parental monitoring, study time, parent/student/teacher contracts, and reward systems.

Begin and end each meeting with a positive and encouraging comment about the child. This technique is known as **P.N.P – POSITIVE–NEGATIVE–POSITIVE**. For example, if a student has been an occasional discipline problem, but has otherwise performed adequately in class, begin the conference by stating a *positive* about the student. Then clearly state the discipline problem *(negative)*, your concern, resolution, and action-step. Conclude the conference with another *positive* comment about the student. In musical terms, the *dissonance is resolved*.

Make notations *following* **the meeting.** Continual writing during a conference tends to make parents feel uncomfortable and afraid to speak up. Carefully record your comments upon completion of the conference and maintain a file on each student. Never include these personal comments in a permanent file, record, or report.

Confrontation

If a parent confronts you regarding procedures or methods, remain calm and address the concern with conviction and rationale. If they continue to converse in an argumentative fashion, state that you *understand their concern* and would be happy to schedule a meeting with the building principal present to discuss the matter further. Under no circumstance should you ever be subjected to *verbal abuse*. If a parent curses at you, calmly state that you will not be spoken to in this manner. If they cannot refrain from using inappropriate language, you should conclude the conversation until a meeting with the principal can be arranged. If the situation escalates, you need to leave and immediately *transcribe* the encounter (dialogue) on paper. Then report directly to your immediate supervisor, informing him/her of the confrontation, and submit a copy of the transcription (keep a copy for your files). You have the right to expect your administrator to work with you and support you in an attempt to resolve the issue.

FUNDRAISING

Because most music budgets are not adequately endowed, it has become customary to raise monies though fundraising. Over ninety percent of high school band directors participate in these efforts, and nearly sixty percent of all budgetary monies are raised through these external crusades. Find out district policy regarding the number of activities in which you can participate. In these days of extensive fundraising, communities can quickly become financially drained. There are, however, many creative ideas that will accomplish your goals while providing the townspeople with worthwhile products and services. You are limited only by your imagination.

You will most likely enter a situation where annual fundraisers are already established. Approach these in the same manner you would any other longstanding tradition: allow them to continue and review the process. If it works, don't reinvent the wheel! Once the fundraising schedule has been determined, delegate the majority of field work to your booster organization. If no booster group exists, recruit parents to spearhead the project. This accomplishes two things: first, your efforts can be concentrated on teaching (not counting boxes of candy bars), and secondly, you relinquish financial and clerical responsibilities. You are better off limiting your involvement to blessing the campaign, making needed administrative contacts, and distributing information to your students.

If for any reason you are required to handle money, keep exact financial records and have a parent or colleague assist in collecting and verifying all accounts. Some directors request a locked container in which money can be placed and opened only by the building principal. Although these precautions may sound overly protective, be assured they are not. You are simply precluding potential problems, and when it comes to money, you want *no questions asked.*

ORGANIZATIONAL PROMOTION

All publicity should be seen as an opportunity to bolster your students and band program. Some booster organizations manage these promotional responsibilities; however, in most cases it is best left to the director. This gives you complete control of the way information is disseminated to the public. Regardless of who handles this job, it must be performed with the utmost of care. Being a good publicist takes organizational skills and the ability to *seize an opportunity*. Just as any good business would advertise its product, the band director must do likewise. Because the majority of publicity will be local, concentrate on the following outlets:

- newspapers
- special editions of the paper
- monthly, quarterly, or semester band newsletter
- area radio stations
- school newspapers
- television

Publicity stories should be *real events* and not an attempt to create something out of nothing. A partial listing of newsworthy items would include:

- the beginning of a new band season
- upcoming performances
- fundraisers
- booster activities/meetings
- trips
- special performances
- upcoming contests and festivals
- honors/awards
- guest soloists/clinicians/directors
- students receiving college scholarships
- camp participants

Most venues are open to presenting your news; however, they will have submission requirements. The following are general guidelines for news releases.

- Typed or computer generated
- Double–spaced
- Correct names, titles, times, and places
- Precise, concise, easy to read, and free from technical jargon
- Answer the questions WHO, WHAT, WHEN, WHERE, and WHY
- Present only the facts; personal opinions should be in the form of quotations
- One to one and one-half pages in length (unless a feature story)
- Title your article (know that it may be changed by the editor)
- Meet all submission deadlines

The following examples will help you frame your press releases.

Royal Heights High School Band

PRESS RELEASE
FOR IMMEDIATE RELEASE

Contact: Mr. Bradley A. Johnson
Director of Bands (417) 625-0008

Concert Band to Perform Spring Concert

May 8, 199_, Royal Heights, MO - The Royal Heights Concert Band, under the direction of Bradley A. Johnson, will perform this Monday, May 14 at 7:30 p.m. in the high school auditorium. This theme concert will feature a patriotic salute to America. Concert selections include *America The Beautiful, Suite of Old American Dances, Marches of America, Torch Of Liberty,* and *Valley Forge.* The concert will conclude with John Philip Sousa's *Stars and Stripes Forever.*

"This concert will be very entertaining," states Mr. Johnson. "The students have learned much about our country by performing these traditional songs of Americana. In addition to rehearsing and preparing the music, we discussed the history of these pieces, making it an interdisciplinary learning experience."

Free transportation will be provided by the Band Boosters to residents of the Leighton Leisure Living Senior Center for this performance. Residents who wish to attend should meet in the front lobby area at 6:45 p.m. Following the concert, the Royal Heights Band Boosters will host a reception in the commons area where re-freshments will be served. The concert is free and open to the public.

Royal Heights High School Band

PRESS RELEASE
FOR IMMEDIATE RELEASE

Contact: Mr. Bradley A. Johnson
Director of Bands (417) 625-0008

Clark Terry to Perform with Jazz Ensemble

May 10, 199_, Royal Heights, MO – Legendary jazz trumpeter **Clark Terry** will serve as guest soloist with the Royal Heights High School Jazz Ensemble as they perform in concert this Wednesday, May 16 at 7:30 p.m. in the high school auditorium. His performance is being sponsored by the Band Boosters and Missouri Arts Council.

World renown jazz musician, Clark Terry, has been described as "a musician beyond category" by famed band leader Duke Ellington. He has played on numerous albums, was inducted into the International Association of Jazz Educators Hall of Fame in 1984, has played with the Duke Ellington Orchestra, Tonight Show Band, Count Basie Orchestra, Quincy Jones Band, as well as his own big band and small groups. He performs concerts throughout the United States and Europe.

"We are fortunate to have Clark Terry as a soloist with our jazz ensemble," stated director Bradley A. Johnson. "We have spent the last two days in rehearsals, and the students have learned a great deal about musicianship and improvisation from Mr. Terry."

The jazz ensemble will be performing a variety of literature including two pieces originally written and arranged for Clark Terry's BIG BAD Band: *Sheba* and *The Flintstones*. In addition, the band will feature the trombone section on a new publication entitled *Groovin' Blues*. The concert is free and open to the public.

Pictures

When submitting photos, be sure to adhere to any publishing pre-requisites. Some newspapers prefer not to print large group pictures but will request action shots of one or two members from the ensemble. Submitted photos should be black and white glossy (color is acceptable) and 3″ x 5″, 4″ x 6″, or 5″ x 7″ in size (a light or white background makes for better print). The following information should be included on the back of submitted photos.

Students Pictured: Ashley Covington (left) and Stephanie Giltner (right).
Please return this photograph to Bradley A. Johnson, Royal Heights Community Schools, 1485 Newman Road, Royal Heights, MO 64801 (SASE attached)

Theme concerts are also good publicity and a wonderful way to create public interest. Possibilities include:

Columbus Day
Thanksgiving
United Nations Day
Election Day
Veteran's Day
Christmas/Hanukkah
Halloween
Lincoln's/Washington's Birthday
Martin Luther King Day
St. Patrick's Day
Easter
Mother's/Father's Day
Memorial Day
Labor Day

The following are examples of possible themes and suggested preparation.

Holiday Concert

- Select a wide range of holiday music to perform (perhaps international works)
- Get everyone involved with audience participation songs
- Have Santa Claus make a surprise visit
- Decorate the stage with lit and garnished Christmas trees
- Serve refreshments at a reception following the concert
- Invite student classes to display their holiday arts and crafts

A Patriotic Theme

- Select an appropriate patriotic program
- Invite community organizations and their auxiliary units to participate or display memorabilia (American Legion, Veterans of Foreign Wars, historical societies, etc.)
- Invite the Color Guard from the Army, Navy, Air Force or Marine service organizations to arrange flag displays

The First Year Blues

Being a band director is one of the most stressful and demanding jobs in the education field. First year blues occur for many reasons, including discipline problems, lack of respect, professional injustices, and fatigue. Are the first year blues inevitable? Perhaps to some degree; however, they do not have to *control* you. The key is to *reduce your stress level.*

Understand that you – not others – are ultimately responsible for the way you feel during this first year. Don't shoot yourself in the foot and then frantically look around for the guilty party! Outside sources don't often help matters, but there will always be complicating external factions. Stress is about *you,* not them. Unfortunately, you cannot *will* these situations to go away; therefore, your goal is to effectively deal with the conditions that cause the *first year blues.*

Hold others accountable. Hold your students accountable for their actions. Don't take their responsibilities and make them your own. When a student approaches you in class stating a problem (i.e. they have no pencil, forgot their music), respond with an accountability question: "What are *you* going to do about that?" or "How are *you* going to solve *your* problem?"

Don't take it home. Make your home a sanctuary, a refuge far removed from the tensions of the day. This time should be reserved for family, friends, hobbies, or just grappling with the hills and valleys of your personal life. In short, this is a time for personal development. A variety of interests outside music and education will actually help strengthen your teaching skills. By caring for your physical, mental, and spiritual well-being, you will be more effective at your work.

Take time each day for yourself. Find fifteen to thirty minutes every day for personal development. Having taught for a number of years, the author is fully aware of the demands placed on you during every school day; however, you must set aside this time. Schedule this interim during your lunch break, a preparation period, or before or after school. This personal break should be void of work related activity. Read a newspaper or magazine, walk around the block, or get a cup of coffee and just relax; the activities will refresh you both mentally and physically.

Don't feel guilty. Oh yes, martyrdom . . . the nicotine of stress! You must stop feeling guilty because you are not working every second, of every minute, of every day, seven days a week. This turns into a vicious cycle, culminating with the belief that you can never do enough for professional edification. For your own self–protection, learn to say NO! During your first year you may be asked to serve on numerous committees, volunteer for school and community functions, etc. Be selective and don't overextend yourself! Memorize this response, "I'm flattered that you would ask; however, I must respectfully decline. My time is allocated." Can you say no without feeling guilty?

Be efficient. Lack of organization causes stress! Each of us has a procedural format, and this is the way it should be; however, realize that you can never *always* be organized, and please . . . don't go overboard. Find a system that works and stick to it.

Be realistic. New directors often inflict unrealistic schedules and goals upon themselves. Write down short and long term goals in *pencil*, and know that as you progress through the year, they will change. If they are not being altered, you are not being very observant. Remember, the only thing constant in life is change, so be realistic and flexible.

Scheduling. Every band program should be active in an educationally-sound manner. However, one cannot help but wonder if a rigorous competition schedule, coupled with unrealistic expectations, are the driving force behind many band programs. Self-inflicted schedules that include before school rehearsals, after school sectionals, evening lessons, and numerous weekend performances are a recipe for burnout. Be very prudent in the performance and rehearsal decisions you make as many issues come into play; one of these includes your *personal well-being*.

Have a positive attitude. If you have not read Norman Vincent Peale's book *The Power of Positive Thinking*, spend the $4.95 and do so. Peale's advice can change your life. Of course you *will* have to deal with negative people during your first year, so make a conscious effort not to get caught up in their pity parties. As a general rule, *insulate* yourself from negative people but don't *isolate*. Save isolationism for those who are meanspirited, and no doubt you will have the opportunity to meet this *cheery* group during your first year!

Learn to laugh. Periodically you must reflect on the important things in your life. Yes, your position as a band director and the well–being of your students are substantial responsibilities; however, don't forget *your* personal needs and goals. The difficulties associated with being a band director can be rather amusing if you put them into perspective. Obviously some are better at seeing the humor in situations than others, but if you wish to reduce your stress level, recognize that almost every situation in life has a lighter side. So laugh! It feels great!

PART FIVE

REHEARSALS & PERFOMANCES

Success is 20% skills and 80% strategy.

— Jim Rohn

Recruiting

During the mid–elementary years (grades 3-4), school music classes usually introduce instruments such as the recorder, auto-harp, and auxiliary percussion as a preface to beginning serious study of a band or orchestral instrument. When this recruitment opportunity presents itself (grades 4-6), students, parents, and directors embark upon an important selection process. The determining factor when recruiting beginning students is your ability to communicate with their parent(s). They make the final decision whether or not their child will have the opportunity to become musically involved. The following guide contains information that should be shared with parents.

Afford them the opportunity. Many children are gifted with a musical sense, but without the opportunity of early training, it may be lost. Research shows that children who participate in music not only increase their aesthetic sensitivities toward the arts and humanities, but also improve comprehension and higher order thinking skills.

Encourage participation. Parents who were not involved in music should not assume their children will have no interest. By showing support for this endeavor, the child will most likely be more responsive.

Knowledge is power. Find out in advance when students in the school district begin playing musical instruments. A telephone call to the elementary band director will yield specific dates. Gather as much information as possible from school officials, friends, and educators. The more informed you are, the better decision you will make.

Talk *to* your children, not *at* them. Discuss the different instruments with your child to determine if they have a sincere interest. If you are not familiar with the musical families, speak to an educator or check out a book from the library. Keep an open ear regarding instruments that seem to intrigue your child the most.

Preclude long-term problems. Consult the elementary band director and a dentist to discuss teeth, embouchure, and facial construction. These physical traits are a consideration when selecting the instrument best suited for your child. By this age (grades 4-6), a dentist can give you a sense of your child's teeth structure and will probably be able to tell if braces are in the future, and to what extent. Braces could make a high brass instrument, such as the trumpet or French horn, a painful choice for several years. If an asthmatic condition is present, a percussion or string instrument may be a better selection.

Visit your local music store. Have a salesperson demonstrate the instruments for you; better yet, have your child hold them and attempt to produce a sound. The actual decision as to which instrument your child selects should be the result of a caucus. Receive input from external sources; however, allow your child to voice an opinion. The most disgruntled and frustrated students are often children whose parents selected the instrument for them. Avoid living your musical fantasies through your child.

A musical instrument is a major investment. New beginner models range from $400.00 to $1,000.00. Rental plans are often available through your local music store, which allow you to lease an instrument for a determined period of time while observing to see if your child has continued interest. If the music store offers repair insurance (usually a nominal fee) in conjunction with the rental, it is worth the investment. Young students tend to be hard on instruments, and restoration can be costly. Used instruments can often be found in the classified ads of a newspaper; however, before making a purchase, take it to a reliable technician to determine its general condition and value. This trained individual will not only give you an estimate of any needed repair but will also tell you if it is an appropriate model for a beginner. In this introductory mode, your child does not need the torment of an instrument that does not work properly. If finances are a concern, check with the school to see if district–owned instruments can be rented.

Private instruction = success. Some music programs offer instrumental lessons; however, if yours does not, private instruction outside of school is a viable and worthwhile option (costs range from $6.00 to $15.00 per half hour). Students who study privately succeed at a higher level and progress faster. A quality instructor is a must, so ask for recommendations from the band director. Accompany your child to the first few lessons so both of you feel comfortable with the instructor's teaching methods.

Support your child's practice. Establish a quiet area away from the telephone and television. Select a practice time when your child has energy, and schedule sessions at the same time every day. Begin with fifteen minutes per day for the first six months, then move incrementally to thirty minutes. Sit with your budding musician as he/she practices. Even if you do not have a musical ear, this gesture shows your support. Gradually allow your child to rehearse on his/her own and visit near the end of the session for an update on progress.

Praise, praise, and more praise! Understand that playing a musical instrument is not an instant–gratification project. It can take up to six months before a child can produce a satisfactory sound. Praise your child daily on their musical progress and savor the experience.

MUSIC SELECTION

Good band literature is subjective; however, there are a host of time–proven pieces that bear the title *exemplary*. Some state organizations provide lists which will assist you in your music selection. There are also prominent guides/articles which catalogue outstanding concert and jazz band literature at the intermediate and advanced levels. Publishers have a standard procedure for grading band material, and although these classifications are rather introspective, they are helpful.

School Level	Literature/Grade Level
Elementary	1 - 1 1/2 - 2
Middle School/Junior High	2 - 2 1/2 - 3
High School	3 - 3 1/2 - 4 - 4 1/2
College/University	4 1/2 - 5 - 5 1/2
Professional	5 1/2 - 6

Some publishers will grade works: very easy, easy, medium, medium difficult, difficult, very difficult.

School Level	Literature/Grade Level
Elementary ·	Very Easy - Easy
Middle School/Junior High	Easy - Medium
High School	Medium Difficult - Difficult
College/Professional	Difficult - Very Difficult

Most publishers are delighted to send you a catalogue of their music along with recorded excerpts (tapes, CDs). Many directors find this to be an effective way to select music; however, don't be mesmerized with the quality of the recording. Allow the music to stand on its own merit without digital enhancement. There are many outstanding pieces of literature on the market, so select musical styles that fit your instrumentation and will allow your band to succeed.

Your first objective is to evaluate your personnel and instrumentation. For example, if your high school band is thirty–five members of which eight are quality percussionists, selecting a Beethoven transcription might not be the best choice. Perhaps a work by Jared Spears or Elliot Del Borgo (two composers who traditionally write interesting and challenging percussion parts) would better suit the ensemble. If you find yourself struggling with the selection process, contact an experienced educator and ask for advice. Avoid the first year trap of choosing material that is too difficult. Attempting to play literature that is beyond the capability of your students is *setting your band up for failure* (there is no educational merit in this type of selection). If you are going to error, error on the side of choosing music that is too easy rather than too difficult.

If you find a piece that will work for your band in every way except a solo part (i.e. eight measure oboe solo and you have no oboist), don't dismiss the work from consideration. Just because the composer scored the solo in this fashion does not mean you cannot perform the piece. Rewrite the part by allowing the context and timbre of the music to dictate the substitution. Directors who have arranging skills can enhance almost any piece of music they select by rescoring to capitalize on their band's strengths.

ENSEMBLE SETUP

Although there are standardized models for setup, there are literally hundreds of possible seating combinations. Your objective is to musically balance your ensemble. The perfectly balanced band does not exist; however, don't allow this revelation to impede your progress as you strive toward your goal. The following considerations need special attention when designing your ensemble seating arrangements:

Seating placement affects balance. Position a dozen trumpets in the middle of the second row of your concert band, and this truth becomes painfully obvious.

Softer instruments need to be heard. Acoustics demand that woodwind instruments be placed in the front of the concert band if they are to be heard.

Analyze the directional properties of sound. Consider the timbrel difference between a bell-front tuba and an upright model. With this in mind, examine each instrument and its respective placement.

Instrumentation should be given specific consideration. Know your band's strengths and weaknesses. For example, if you have six tenor saxophones in a concert band of forty, chances are the woodwind tenor voice is going to be heavy. If it is not possible to have two or three of these students switch instruments, experiment with their placement, listening for balance and blend.

Know the acoustics of the performance center. Just because a setup works in the rehearsal room does not guarantee a proper balance and blend in the performing area. Get an acoustical *feel* for the room and make needed adjustments. Don't be afraid to experiment; however, avoid making changes days prior to a concert, as students must have ample time to adjust aural perspectives.

Concert band or wind ensemble. Are these titles synonymous? Although some believe a *band is a band,* there is a difference between the ensembles. Size is the major distinction between the two groups although there are numerous literature considerations. A true wind ensemble will consist of thirty–five to forty players and produce a more chamber-like sound. The ensemble is made up of one player on a part; however, because the woodwinds tend to be overshadowed by the brass and percussion, some directors will double these parts. The symphonic or concert band is larger in size and able to produce massive blocks of sound. Of course these numbers may vary depending upon the conductor's musical taste and availability of instrumentalists (Del Borgo 1984, 94).

The following are examples of ensemble setup options.

Symphonic/Concert Band
(Bessom, Tatarunis, and Forcucci 1980, 281)

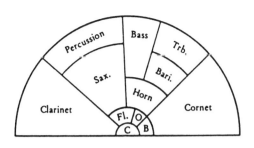

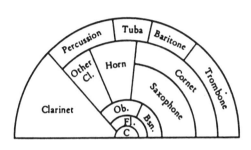

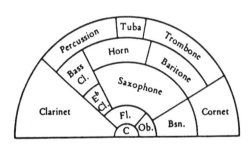

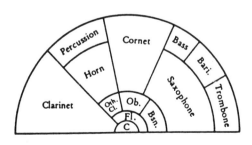

Wind Ensemble
(Bessom, Tatarunis, and Forcucci 1980, 282)

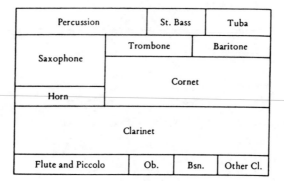

Jazz Ensemble
(Kuzmich and Bash 1984, 35)

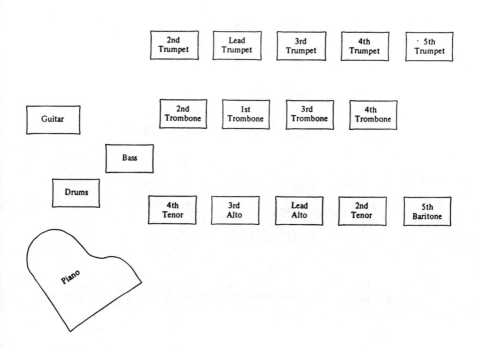

Parade Marching

BRASS or WOODWINDS
(*SCORE ORDER*)
PERCUSSION
BRASS or WOODWINDS
(*SCORE ORDER*)
DRUM MAJOR(S)
COLOR GUARD

PERCUSSION
BRASS or WOODWINDS
(*SCORE ORDER*)
BRASS or WOODWINDS
(*SCORE ORDER*)
DRUM MAJOR(S)
COLOR GUARD

Pep Band

PERCUSSION
LOW BRASS
WOODWINDS
HIGH BRASS

BRASS		
WOODWINDS		
ELEC. BASS	DRUMS	GUITAR

ORGANIZING REHEARSAL TIME

Preparation, organization, and preclusion . . . have you read these words before? Know exactly what you want to accomplish during each rehearsal session. Time wasted could be time spent teaching! The following are a few of the more obvious ways to organize rehearsal time.

Schedule a five minute warm–up at the beginning of each rehearsal. A well planned warm-up session is a learning experience that can teach tone production, listening skills, intonation, balance/blend, sightreading, phrasing, articulations, and dynamic contrast. There are a number of outstanding warm–up books on the market that feature chorales, scales, and technical studies.

Assign roll tasks. Provide a seating chart to a responsible student and have them take attendance while you are giving announcements or warming up the band.

Anticipate problems. This is accomplished through proper score study and knowledge of instrumental pedagogy. Brass, woodwind, and percussion technique courses teach you the intricacies of each wind and percussion instrument, thus permitting you to foresee potential problems. For example, if the score reveals the trumpet section sustaining a unison low D for six measures, you should immediately anticipate intonation problems.

Require a pencil at every rehearsal. Second only to a beautiful-ly balanced band performing quality literature, is the sound of a pencil *clicking* on the stand after being used (it may be advanta-geous to keep a box of pencils in the front of the bandroom).

Recruit a student librarian. Procure a responsible band student to serve as music librarian. This will save you hours of time sorting and filing music and free you for other more important duties.

Post a rehearsal itinerary. Have the rehearsal order written on the board when students enter the bandroom. This allows your band time to place their music in sequence and alleviates the continual search for parts.

Simplify score reading. New directors often have difficulty perusing all staves of the score at one time. The use of a highlighting system will immediately draw your attention to important areas: blue to emphasize dynamic markings, yellow to draw attention to articulations, and pink to address tempo changes. This method allows you to peripherally view a color, relay its meaning to your band, and keep eye contact with your ensemble. Using this system, or variations thereof, will save you hours of having to reexamine score markings.

Verbal remarks must be short and to the point. If you drone on and on about a concept, you waste valuable time and your students will become restless. However, don't confuse verbal brevity with the need for a fast paced rehearsal. Although it is advantageous to keep your session moving, allow your individual style to dictate pace. For example, if you stop the band because the trombone section is not playing legato and the timpani entered two measures early, cut the band off and respond, "Timpani (or student name), you entered two measures early, count carefully; trombones, work to play more legato, remember the DO–DO–DO syllables needed for legato articulation. Everyone, let's begin at measure forty–seven working to correct these problems." By being short and to the point you save time, accomplish more, and reduce potential discipline problems. Stay off your soapbox!

SIGHTREADING

When you hear an outstanding band, it is a sure bet that the program curriculum includes extensive sightreading. Although it is not necessary to read during every rehearsal, schedule periodic sessions. The key to finding time to sightread is to select performance literature that can be prepared in three to six weeks. As a general rule, a high school band should be able to sightread (beginning to end) a piece without completely falling apart in the second or third reading. If they are unable to do this, the work is probably too difficult and should not be programmed. At the elementary or middle school/junior high level, allow three to five reads to complete the piece (beginning to end). This indicates that the work is technically playable with ample rehearsal. All too often directors choose material that is too difficult, thus causing a musical horserace to the concert deadline, leaving little time for the presentation of new concepts (i.e. sightreading).

Have separate sightreading folders that your band librarian can pass out prior to rehearsal, and then later collect and refile. When beginning to read a piece, talk through it step by step, pointing out potential trouble spots, key changes, repeat signs, meter changes, etc. After a few months you will find that learners no longer need to be guided in their search for these musical concepts; simply allot them sixty seconds to mentally prepare. You will be amazed at how quickly your student musicians will progress with scheduled sightreading as part of the curriculum.

OUTSIDE REHEARSALS

Many times jazz ensemble, chamber ensembles, sectionals, and additional marching band rehearsals are scheduled before and/or after school. When programming these outside rehearsals you must ask yourself: Will the additional time commitment cause student burnout? Will it conflict with other school activities? Will administration need to approve such a mandate? What are the short and long term effects of such a decision? The following are additional issues to consider when planning these practice sessions.

• Be sure that students and parents are aware of additional time commitments prior to enrolling.

- Outside scheduling at the elementary and middle school/junior high level should be kept at a minimum, as students are unable to drive and must rely upon parental transportation.

- Give proper notice by posting the rehearsals and listing them in your band handbook (when possible).

- Send a copy of your outside rehearsal schedule to your principal. Should questions arise, all parties have been informed in advance.

- Grades 4-8 should be given a note to take home indicating rehearsal times.

- Keep close tabs on the tenor of student conversation before and after rehearsals. This will be a good indicator if you are overscheduling.

- Encourage section leaders (high school level) to hold outside rehearsals without your assistance.

PRINTED PROGRAMS

There are numerous ways to construct a concert program; however, all should include a cover page, program selection page, personnel page, and back page. The following is an example.

Royal Heights Community Schools
presents

THE
ROYAL HEIGHTS MIDDLE SCHOOL

7th and 8th Grade

Concert Band

Bradley A. Johnson, Director

Auditorium
Royal Heights Middle School
February 21, 199_
7:30 p.m.

Program Selections

Richland Overture	John O'Reilly
A Hymn For Band	Hugh M. Stuart
Fanfare Prelude on "Finlandia"	Jean Sibelius arr. Jim Curnow
Administrative Remarks	Mr. Thomas E. Davis
Introduction and Caccia	Claude T. Smith
A Western Portrait	Pierre La Plante
Liberty Fleet	Karl L. King

Personnel

Piccolo:
Kexi Liu

Flute:
Tuam Alam
Jennifer Bragg
Sarah Butler *
Hollie Cullinan
Mackenzie Hilfers
Monica Hohn
Ruth Mack

Oboe:
Jennifer Vogt

Bassoon:
Jason DeYoung
Gina Walter *

Clarinet:
Kim Berg
Stacy Gilland
Jeni Gruwell
Ron Houk
Cybil Johnson
James Morphew
Sarah Overturf *

Bass Clarinet:
Terri McDavitt *
Mike Nelson

Alto Saxophone:
Cara DeMoss
Todd Essick *
Mike Green

Tenor Saxophone:
Curt Hopkins
Chad Parker *

Baritone Saxophone:
Jaime Fontana *
Ray St. Ledger

Trumpet:
Darin Dowling
Matt Huddleston *
Eric Johnston
Ryan Meyers
Derek Nestor
Martin O'Hara

French Horn:
Derek Anfinson
Holly Brinegar
Erika Ellis
Shannon Kershaw *

Trombone:
John Burger *
Brent Myers
Jeff Pigg
Jose Wasinga

Euphonium:
Tonya Harrod
Matt Stauffer *

Tuba:
Matt Bresh *
Geoff Meyer

Percussion:
Kristen Carlson
Bud Clark *
Mindy Haverhals

* denotes section leader

Spell all names correctly, as parents and students are troubled if misspellings or omissions occur. Circulate a draft program to your students to ensure that their names are listed correctly. Should an error inadvertently appear in the printed program, publicly acknowledge the oversight and recognize the individual(s) in question during the concert. In addition, your personnel page should list students in alphabetical order (by instrument), not in order of chair or part placement. This signifies that each student and the part they play are of equal importance, thus eliminating any potential awkward feelings on the part of students and parents. Denoting section leaders or principal chair players can be accomplished by placing an asterisk after the name.

(Back Page)

Royal Heights Community School Officials

Richard Geith	Superintendent
Deanna Matheney	Administrative Assistant
Thomas E. Davis	Middle School Principal

Band Booster Executives

Leonard Bonker	President
Charles Thelen	Vice President
Reginald Witherspoon	Secretary
Rebecca Martins	Treasurer

Special Thanks

Elizabeth Lovland	Bernard Allgood
Pete Havely	Jena Hawk
Gary Granneman	Wesley Smith
Royal Heights Band Booster Members	

Upcoming Band Events

March 20	District Solo/Ensemble Contest
April 10	Band Fun Night Concert
May 6	State Large Group Contest
May 14	Concert Band Spring Concert
May 16	Jazz Ensemble Concert
May 29	Tulip Festival Parade

Options for your back page could include upcoming events, future concerts, fine arts schedule, recognitions, honors, executive booster members, administration, etc. Use this page to your advantage – DON'T LEAVE IT BLANK!

Program notes are optional. It is sometimes difficult to find historical information on newly composed band pieces; in this event, a short overview of the musical aspects of the work will suffice.

Fanfare Prelude on "Finlandia"   Jean Sibelius arr. Jim Curnow
The career of Jean Sibelius was most explicitly nationalistic in his orchestral and choral works. During the 1890's he produced a series of symphonic poems that captured the spirit of Finnish legends and myths. The best known of these is *Finlandia* (1899) from which the melody for this Fanfare Prelude is taken.

A Western Portrait   Pierre La Plante
A Western Portrait is based on two old cowboy tunes. The slow sections, at the beginning and end, are based on *All Day On The Prairie*. It is a lonely melody that suggests an aspect of life on the plains. The fast movement is based on *The Old Chisolm Trail*. It starts as a call to "head 'em up and move 'em out" and turns into a "hoedown" motif. Pierre La Plante is an active composer and currently serves as Director of Bands at Pecatonica Area Schools in Blanchardville, Wisconsin.

An option to printed notes is to secure a narrator. This adds a personal touch to the concert and affords you an opportunity to invite a colleague, administrator, or community member to serve in this capacity.

Narration Excerpt

Good evening ladies and gentlemen and welcome to the annual spring concert of the Royal Heights High School Concert Band under the direction of Mr. Bradley A. Johnson. The opening selection was *The Klaxon March* by Henry Fillmore. This march was composed in 1929 and published the next year. The work was originally subtitled March of the Automobiles because it was written for the Cincinnati Automobile Show which began at the Music Hall in January of 1930. This composition sparked Fillmore to invent a new instrument for the occasion; he called it the Klaxophone. It consisted of twelve multi–pitched automobile horns mounted on a table and powered by a car battery. We chose to perform the modern version – minus klaxophone (Smith and Stoutamire 1979, 72).

The band's next selection, *Roman Carnival Overture* was composed by Hector Berlioz and is based on themes from the opera Benvenuto Cellini. The opening dance from the second act, and Bevenuto's love theme from the first, are two of the melodies prominently featured. The opera itself was not very successful, but this overture has proven to be an attractive performance excerpt. The premiere performance took place in Paris on February 3, 1844 under the conductor's personal direction. It pleased the audience so greatly on this occasion that it had to be repeated. The chief thematic material of the overture is taken directly from the score of the opera and has been skillfully arranged for wind band by Erik Leidzen. We hope you enjoy *Roman Carnival Overture* (Smith and Stoutamire 1979, 27).

CONCERT ETIQUETTE

It is crucial that you present yourself and your band in a professional manner. Although some of the procedures listed may seem elementary, memorize and follow these recommendations.

Proper attire. If your concert band performs in a uniform, you should wear a black tuxedo, white shirt, and bow tie. If your ensemble wears dress clothes, you then have the option of wearing a tuxedo or dark colored formal wear. Avoid accessories or any jewelry that could be disruptive to the audience or musicians.

Entering and exiting the stage. Make sure you have a clear path upon which to enter and wait until you have reached center stage before you acknowledge the applause of the audience with a formal bow. Staging and logistics will dictate your band's entrance; however, percussionists should enter first as they need additional time to arrange equipment.

Teach proper positioning. Proper sitting position is on the front half of the chair with feet flat on the floor. Instrument *resting, ready* and *playing* positions are indicated by physical cues: when you *stand next* to the podium, instruments are in a resting position; when you *stand on* the podium, instruments are in a ready position, and when your *baton is raised*, instruments move to a playing position. When these concepts are instilled during rehearsals, proper positioning becomes second nature.

Accepting applause. Always accept applause by bowing to the audience and then gesturing with your arm toward your band, transferring the recognition. Following a feature or concert finale, be sure your band members stand immediately and accept the applause. The exception to this instantaneous movement is when recognition is given to a soloist prior to the entire band.

Recognizing soloist(s). Immediately following a piece which features a principal soloist, recognize the student by pointing to them and having them stand (jot a note at the end of the score to remind yourself to do this). Soloist recognition in a jazz ensemble is accomplished in the same manner. This gesture informs the audience that the solo has ended, and they are free to applaud the improvisation.

Tune *prior* to the concert. Avoid tuning the band in front of the audience – especially instrument by instrument. Even the least discerning audience member will recognize weaknesses under these circumstances. If your band has had to wait an extended period of time prior to entering the stage, allow them an onstage warm–up (not directed) consisting of randomly played notes and scales. This is followed by your principal clarinetist playing a concert pitch for final tuning. Once tuning is complete you should make your entrance.

The downbeat must be clear. Avoid *counting off* your concert band. The solution is to have the band breathe with you at the speed of the preparatory beat as this indicates the proper tempo. Counting off a jazz ensemble or pep band is acceptable.

Conduct with the baton. Avoid tapping your foot while conducting. It looks ridiculous, it is noisy, and it creates two sources of tempo.

Demand proper behavior. Don't allow your students to create any kind of distraction during the concert. This includes visible reactions when mistakes are made.

You are under no obligation to *tell–all*. Never apologize to the audience for music you are about to play or have just performed poorly. By saying "We haven't had much time to rehearse this next piece, but we are going to play it anyway," tells your audience exactly what is going to happen: a poor performance. There is also no need to report that "Mary is missing because . . . she is sick . . . had to work . . . had a volleyball match." If the piece cannot be played correctly without Mary, or the part covered by another player, *just don't play the piece.* Avoid performing music that is not adequately prepared. You are not bound by law to perform every selection listed on the program.

End on a good note. Never dismiss the audience at the conclusion of a concert. Your printed program clearly informs them when it is over. If you don't use a program, then announce your final selection and thank the audience for their participation. Concerts that are too long can never end on a good note! Rule of thumb: always leave your audience wanting more (McKee 1989, 16).

CONCERT RECEPTIONS

A reception following a concert is an ideal time for performers, parents, and audience members to celebrate a successful evening, informally socialize, and enjoy the fruits of their labor. This is also the perfect opportunity for your booster organization to become actively involved by organizing this event. Avoid assuming any responsibilities during this evening, as you will be far too busy with performance duties. Below is a checklist that you will need to consider.

- Hold the reception in an area large enough to accommodate everyone.

- Clear all aspects of this event with your building principal.

- Place all setup requests in writing to the maintenance staff well in advance of the event (be sure to invite them to the concert and reception).

- Commission the boosters to select the types and quantity of food needed. Empowerment in this case refers to transference of responsibilities.

- Announce the reception in your concert program and verbally invite the audience prior to performing your final selection.

GUEST SOLOIST/CLINICIAN

The primary reason to have a guest soloist perform with your ensemble is for the musical benefit of your students. If you are looking for a way to spark enthusiasm, this is a viable option. A myriad of techniques and musicalities can be learned from these guests. If budget is a concern, as it usually is, invite area college professors to solo with your ensemble, for this affords them the opportunity to make an appearance on behalf of their institution.

Additional considerations are as follows:

Check with area directors for recommendations. This is perhaps the best way to determine if a soloist/clinician is effective. It would be wonderful to bring in a *headliner* every year, but unfortunately, it is a bit unrealistic. Therefore your goal is to hire the very finest individual available who will work within the confines of your budget.

Select an educationally–based soloist/clinician. A professional performer does not inherently make a good teacher; these are two distinct professions. Regardless of how outstanding the performer might be, if they are unable to effectively communicate and share their knowledge with your students, then you have wasted time and money.

Publicize the event. Request a biography of your guest and use your public relation skills to promote the concert. If you are initiating the effort to commission a soloist, put forth a similar effort to draw people to the performance.

The one day invitation. Scheduling an area director, who is a master teacher, to work with your band is a wonderful experience for both you and your students. These one day clinicians usually require only a small stipend and can accomplish much in a short amount of time.

FESTIVALS

There are numerous educationally–sound reasons to attend music festivals. However, of primary consideration should be the adjudicator(s), guest director(s), and/or clinician(s). They should be master teachers who are competent in evaluation and who possess an educational approach to the festival venue. These events should be positive learning experiences; however, let the fun be the result of achieving a goal and a job well done.

You will most likely inherit festivals (some competative) which the band has participated in for many years. Gauge your evaluation of these longstanding traditions carefully as administration, student, parent, and community expectations can be very high. To compete or not to compete is a question only you can answer based upon your educational philosophy. This does not have to be an either–or situation. You may wish to compete in a few contests and perform in noncompetitive festivals as well. Before submitting your festival application form, ask yourself if the event meets the educational needs of your students.

Some directors incorporate a student evaluation assignment which all band members are required to complete while attending music festivals. Students are instructed to listen and evaluate three bands during the day and submit their review for a grade. The author strongly advocates this participatory form of learning. The following outlines the assignment.

Festival Evaluation

Tone quality. When students play, do you hear expressive tone qualities? Describe these sounds. Did you hear any vibrato?

Intonation. Did students tune before playing? If so, what approach did they use? Did the ensemble play in tune?

Balance and blend. Did the ensemble blend well or did certain parts stick out? Could the melody or solo parts be heard?

Articulation. Did students articulate clearly and together?

Attacks, releases, and phrases. Did students enter and release at the same time? Did the ensemble phrase together?

Control of tempo and dynamic range. Were the students able to maintain tempos? Did the ensemble perform with a wide range of dynamics?

Rhythmic and technical accuracy. Was the performance free of wrong notes and rhythms?

General musicianship. Were the students dressed appropriately for a public performance? Did they have good posture, instrument position, and hand position? Did they do something while performing that you have never seen or heard before? Reflect on your general impression of the performance.

SUMMER MUSIC CAMPS.

There are many solvent reasons to encourage your students to attend a summer music camp. However, one of the keys to promoting the right camp is matching the student's educational needs to the camp's opportunities. The more information you have, the better recommendation you will make. The following guide presents criteria for making these important endorsements.

Determine the camp's philosophy. Each camp tends to promote a specific ideology. Even ones that provide multiple options for participants (concert band, jazz ensemble, theory, etc.) tend to advocate an established mission. Glean as much information as you can from the brochure, realizing that you will have to speak to former participants, camp coordinators, and area directors to evaluate the camp's specific axiom.

Instructors and faculty. It is crucial that you know who the teachers are, their backgrounds, and experience. Most camps offer excellent faculty; however, some clinicians are not adept in dealing with young musicians. Camps should include distinguished, educationally–grounded faculty who represent diverse educational and professional experiences.

Organization is paramount. Organization on the part of the camp director is crucial to making your students' experience a positive one. Realize that there are a few camps which *fly–by–night*, with the primary goal of making money. This is the exception rather than the rule. You have very little control over the organizational structure, yet you can preclude a negative experience by recommending other camps.

The cost factor. Tuition varies greatly, and participants should be informed in advance of any additional costs that will be incurred. Fees may not include room and board! Transportation costs and refund for cancellation policies should be made clear. Deliberate the total cost package versus the educational merit.

Scholarships. These are not always announced or promoted in the brochures. Scholarships are usually presented on the basis of musical merit or financial need. If this is a consideration for your students, contact the camp director and discuss possible grant opportunities.

Scheduling is key. Good camps tend to present a full day of events with a variety of offerings and classes interspersed in the schedule. Residencies that include evening performances by guest clinicians and camp faculty receive high praise. Avoid offerings that require students to be in extended single ensemble rehearsals (i.e. 9:00 a.m. to 11:30 a.m. followed by a 1:00 p.m. to 3:30 p.m. rehearsal). This type of itinerary can become monotonous and counterproductive. It is also important that students are allotted some free time for social development.

Audition procedures. Most auditions take place during the first day. This is done so participants can be placed in a group that best meets their needs. You should know what material will be used for the audition, adjudication criteria, and then prepare your students for the experience. Let's face it, auditions can be frightening! Inquiry into these procedures should help preclude undue concern.

The following items are of special importance to parents.

Housing considerations. Because most camps are held on college campuses, participants are usually housed in dormitory settings. Answers to the following questions are essential: Will college students be in the dorms during this time? Are the dorms coed? Will campers be housed in a specific wing of a building? Are participants housed by age, grade level, or instrumentation? How many students per room? Is single housing available, and at what additional cost? Also, request a layout of the housing unit prior to the camp so students are aware of emergency exits.

Inquire into meal services. Camps held at colleges often offer a variety of foods, including vegetarian and dietary options. Inquire if additional costs will be incurred for these alternatives. Refrigerator and microwave service may also be important to students with specific medical or health related diets.

Security is a serious consideration. Find out who is in charge of supervision, curfew times, and where instruments are housed. Also be sure your student(s) and their parent(s) are given information regarding area medical clinics and hospitals.

Final concert performance. Most camps offer a concluding performance in which family and friends are invited. If at all possible, attend this showing and listen to your students' efforts. This will give you a better understanding upon which to base future recommendations and will also lend support to your participants.

Music camps not only help learners become better musicians, but better people. They tend to raise performance levels, systemically promoting esprit de corps throughout your entire band. Encourage your student musicians to attend an educationally-grounded summer music camp, and everyone involved will reap the benefits. Comprehensive camp guides are listed annually in many professional journals (indexed in appendix).

PART SIX

ACQUIRING THE JOB

The most important question to ask on the job is not "What am I getting?" but rather "What am I becoming?"

— Jim Rohn

THE RESUME

Constructing a resume is a demanding and time consuming task; therefore, you must initiate the process months prior to beginning your job search. College students should start drafting materials at the beginning of the senior year. If you delay the proceeding until you are in the midst of your student teaching experience, you will find yourself too involved to adequately fulfill these requirements.

A resume is a concise, one or two-page summary of your background and experiences. Since employers rarely spend more than twenty seconds when first scanning a resume, your information must be a highlight of your qualifications, not a life history. It will compete with possibly hundreds of other applications and therefore, must be exact. Experienced administrators have assessed numerous vitae over the span of their careers and will be quite critical when reviewing your materials. Construct a resume that outlines your capabilities, grabs the reader's attention, and is grammatically perfect.

To create a successful resume, you should have a keen awareness of your values, interests, abilities, skills, strengths, and weaknesses. Although it is not often we inflict this self–analysis upon ourselves, it is time to toss modesty and inhibition aside and boldly state marketable qualities. Your resume becomes your sales pitch – a marketing tool! It is your ticket to a personal interview. On a scale of 1 – 10 (10 being the highest), evaluate yourself.

Organizational Skills	____
Decision Making	____
Evaluation	____
Planning	____
Problem Solving	____
Scheduling	____
Adapting	____
Creating	____
Analyzing	____

Coordinating ____
Directing/Conducting ____
Goal Setting ____
Guidance ____
Leadership Skills ____
Motivating ____
Persuading ____
Listening ____
Speaking ____
Writing ____
Musical Performance ____
Relationships ____

Additional Strengths:

_____

_____

_____

_____

Once you have completed this appraisal, list your top five proficiencies. This will serve as a foundation upon which to frame your resume and cover letter.

1. _____
2. _____
3. _____
4. _____
5. _____

FORMAT

Your resume must be an honest reflection of you. It should state your personal and professional strengths and accentuate your abilities to successfully perform the job. The following outline represents a traditional format.

Heading. Include your full name (middle initial is acceptable), home/campus address, zip code, and all telephone numbers where you wish to be contacted. Place this information in a prominent position at the top of the resume.

BRADLEY A. JOHNSON

319 Meadowlark Lane, Apt. 14 C
Royal Heights, Missouri 64801
417-625-0000 home
417-625-0008 work

Employment objective. Although this portion of the resume is optional, it affords you an opportunity to impress the employer with a dynamic soundbite. This written objective should be one. or two carefully worded sentences which answer the following questions: What do I want to do? and What personal qualities will enable me to do it? An example of an employment objective, or professional profile as it is sometimes called, is presented below.

EMPLOYMENT OBJECTIVE:

> Versatile, goal-oriented music instructor with a B.S. in music education who can provide a sound learning environment while using innovative teaching techniques to encourage active student participation.

Professional skills. Introducing these character traits will project self-confidence and highlight relevant qualifications. These attributes can be obtained from the self-evaluation you completed at the beginning of this section. This category is also optional.

PROFESSIONAL SKILLS:

Exhibits excellent supervisory skills.
Displays strong planning and organizational abilities.
Communicates effectively and works cooperatively with students, colleagues, and public.
Treats all people fairly and with respect.

Education. Include the full name of the educational institution and accurate dates of attendance. Identify all degrees granted and list any academic honors such as cum laude, Dean's list, G.P.A. (3.0 or above only).

EDUCATION:

BACHELOR OF SCIENCE
Music Education, Missouri Southern State College
Joplin, Missouri May, 199_. (G.P.A. 3.42)

Career related experience. List all pertinent details of related work experience. This indicates to the employer that you have met responsibilities in an occupational setting.

CAREER RELATED EXPERIENCE:

Student Teacher   March 199_ - May 199_
International School of Missouri, Royal Heights, MO
Mr. Carl W. Knox, Cooperating Teacher
Organized and incorporated learning strategies for 160 student musicians (approximately 35% international students) in a large group band setting. Successfully rehearsed and conducted chamber ensembles at state small group contest. Coordinated and taught instructional group lessons.

Work Study Employee   September 199_ to present
Missouri Southern State College, Joplin, MO
Music Department
Corrected examinations and entered scores into mainframe computer. Entrusted with confidential files of over 100 students. Proctored 25 student makeup examinations.

Data Entry Operator   June 199_ to present
Wells Dairy, Inc., Joplin, MO
Computer entry of various financial accounts ranging from small grocery stores to large distributors. Trained 22 employees in computer accounts and billing files.

Honors and activities. Administrators are interested in your honors and activities, both in and out of the classroom. These commendations show the employer that you are well–rounded and self-motivated. Positions of leadership are especially impressive. Academic honors may be listed here or in the education section.

HONORS AND ACTIVITIES:

> Education Academic Fellow
> Mu Sigma Music Society
> Alpha Chi National Honor Society
> Dean's List
> Teacher Education Committee
> College Music Educators National Conference, Chapter
>   Vice President

Personal data. Any personal data you wish to enter should be placed at the end of the resume. Information regarding height, weight, marital status, and race need not be included. In addition, the author does not recommend using a photo resume. You want to be evaluated on your qualifications, not your physical features.

References. These are qualified individuals who can attest to your abilities and skills. Select references carefully and well in advance of your employment search. Ask potential referrals if they would feel comfortable serving in such a capacity. Once you have secured three to five endorsements, contact your college/university career placement office for further assistance. If you choose to list references as part of your resume, do so on a separate page. Enter the individual's full name, title, business address, and telephone number(s).

REFERENCES

Albert J. Carnine, D.M.A.
Professor of Music, Missouri Southern State College
9850 Logan Drive
Joplin, Missouri 64801
Home   (417) 625-5555
Work   (417) 626-6666

There are many creative ways to construct your resume. Whichever method you select, consider the following information:

Printing. The resume must be balanced, neat, easy to read, and placed on 8 1/2" x 11" quality paper. A white or off–white textured bond (25 lb. rag) is recommended.

Organization. Your information should be structured in an attractive and marketable format. The employer will view the arrangement of your resume as a direct reflection of your organizational skills.

Sequence. Arrange the information in a logical, easy to follow, sequential order. Dated items are usually placed in reverse chronological order.

Length. Limit your resume to one or two pages. Longer curriculum vitae are acceptable if your employment experience is extensive or greater academic preparation is required (this is usually not the case for the new director).

Writing style. Avoid wordiness and repetition; strive for conciseness. Use phrases instead of lengthy sentences and incorporate action words.

Format. Readability, eye appeal, and a positive impression should be format goals. Generous spacing and separation of the components will help you achieve this effect. Bold key headings will also enhance the organizational *look*. Absolutely no grammatical errors are allowed!

BRADLEY A. JOHNSON

319 Meadowlark Lane, Apt. 14 C
Royal Heights, Missouri 64801
417-625-0000 home
417-625-0008 work

EMPLOYMENT OBJECTIVE:

Versatile, goal-oriented music instructor with a B.S. in music education
who can provide a sound learning environment while using innovative
teaching techniques to encourage active student participation.

PROFESSIONAL SKILLS:

Exhibits excellent supervisory skills.
Displays strong planning and organizational abilities.
Communicates effectively and works cooperatively with students,
colleagues, and public.
Treats all people fairly and with respect.

EDUCATION:

BACHELOR OF SCIENCE
Music Education, Missouri Southern State College,
Joplin, Missouri May, 199_. (G.P.A. 3.42)

CAREER RELATED EXPERIENCE:

Student Teacher   March 199_ - May 199_
International School of Missouri, Royal Heights, MO
Mr. Carl W. Knox, Cooperating Teacher
Organized and incorporated learning strategies for 160 student
musicians (approximately 35% international students) in a large
group band setting. Successfully rehearsed and conducted
chamber ensembles at state small group contest. Coordinated
and taught instructional group lessons.

Work Study Employee   September 199_ - to present
Missouri Southern State College, Joplin, MO
Music Department
Corrected examinations and entered scores into mainframe
computer. Entrusted with confidential files of over 100 students.
Proctored 25 student makeup examinations.

Data Entry Operator   June 199_ to present
Wells Dairy, Inc., Joplin, MO
Computer entry of various financial accounts ranging from small
grocery stores to large distributors. Trained 22 employees in
computer accounts and billing files.

HONORS AND ACTIVITIES:

Education Academic Fellow
Mu Sigma Music Society
Alpha Chi National Honor Society
Dean's List
Teacher Education Committee
College Music Educators National Conference,
  Chapter Vice President

REFERENCES

Albert J. Carnine, D.M.A.
Professor of Music
Missouri Southern State College
9850 Logan Drive
Joplin, Missouri 64801
Home   (417) 625-5555
Office (417) 626-6666

William T. Elliott
Professor of Music
Missouri Southern State College
9850 Logan Drive
Joplin, Missouri 64801
Home   (417) 626-0001
Office   (417) 626-0002

Carl W. Knox
Director of Bands
International School of Missouri
357 Albia Road
Joplin, MO 64802
Home   (417) 626-0660
Office   (417) 626-6729

Norma L. Noland
Director of Bands
Fairfield Community High School
89 Connia Street
Fairfield, MO 64871
Home   (417) 628-8566
Office   (417) 628-7334

COVER LETTER

The cover letter creates a first impression. This formal letter accompanies your resume, introduces you to the employer, and indicates your interest in the position. Although there are many ways to compose a letter of application, the following are general guidelines:

- Briefly describe yourself, your skills, and your interest in the educational institution and specific job.

- Attract the employer by offering something. State that your expertise will be valuable in meeting the school's needs.

- Address your letter to a specific person. If no name is listed in the placement ad, call to find out who is heading the position search.

- Compose a brief, businesslike, interesting, perfectly typed or computer generated letter and sign in black ink. Letters of application should never be duplicated.

Bradley A. Johnson

319 Meadowlark Lane, Apt. 14 C
Royal Heights, Missouri 64801
(417) 625-0000 home

May 25, 199_

Mr. Thomas E. Davis
Principal, Royal Heights High School
1485 Newman Road
Royal Heights, MO 64801

Dear Mr. Davis:

First paragraph. State the reason for the letter, the position you are applying for, and specify from which resource (placement center, news media, employment service) you learned of the opening.

Second paragraph. Indicate why you are interested in the job, and what you can do for the employer. If you are a recent graduate, explain how your academic background has prepared you. Highlight related experiences and accomplishments as well as personal traits that qualify you for the position. Try not to repeat the same information the reader will find in the resume.

Final paragraph. Refer the employer to the enclosed resume which summarizes specific qualifications, training, and experiences. Indicate your desire for a personal interview and your flexibility as to the meeting time and place. Be sure to thank the employer for their consideration of your application.

Sincerely,

Bradley A. Johnson

(Enclosure)

THE INTERVIEW

Every interview will be a unique and exhilarating experience. When you are called for this all–important conference, request a verbal itinerary. Some schools will only require a short thirty–minute meeting with an administrator, while others may schedule sessions with the superintendent, principal, school board, and community members, as well as have you teach a lesson. Find out with whom you will meet, the length of the interview, and if you need to prepare specific materials. Gather as much information about the process as possible, and then begin to research the school district. Perhaps the debate team won a state tournament last spring or the band participated in the St. Louis Six Flags Music Festival. This information provides insight, supplies conversational material, and permits you to ask perceptive questions.

You must portray the appearance of a successful, positive, ambitious, and competent music educator. There is only one way to dress for an interview: *conservatively*. Men should wear a dark suit, white shirt, and dark polished shoes and women a stylish pant suit or dress (length below the knee) adding a sense of style with jewelry, a belt, or scarf. Hair must be neat and attractive and never flamboyant. Take a briefcase with supportive materials (i.e. discipline policy, sample lesson plans, philosophy statement etc.) to the interview (Foxman 1989, 171-172).

Your enthusiasm can be shown by a firm handshake and a smile during your greeting. Work to make the employer feel comfortable around you; however, don't assume that you are or can be a personal friend, for this is a business relationship. The interview should be conversational in style, allowing the interviewer to take the *verbal lead*. It is a mistake to ramble on in an attempt to sell (oversell) yourself. Never criticize anyone or anything during an interview. Be positive and encouraging, while always speaking truthfully. If a question is posed in a manner which may prompt you to respond negatively . . . DON'T! Put a *spin* on your answer and make it positive. Complete the interview with a firm handshake, while thanking the interviewer for the opportunity to meet. State your continued interest in the position and inquire when a final decision is expected.

Role play with a friend to practice your interview responses. Rehearse tonal inflection and be brief with your answers. You wouldn't perform a recital without first preparing the material; neither should you expect to hold a successful interview with ad libitum responses. Employers will quickly realize that you are ill–prepared and promptly eliminate you as a finalist for the position. Study the following questions and formulate solvent responses for each.

1. What is the role of the teacher in the classroom?
2. What principles do you use to motivate students?
3. What are your career goals five years from now? Ten years?
4. State a behavioral objective you taught during your student teaching experience.
5. What is the most exciting thing happening in the area of education today?
6. During your student teaching experience, what did you find to be the toughest aspect of discipline?
7. Describe the physical appearance of your classroom.
8. How do you individualize learning in your classes?
9. What rules have you established for your classroom?
10. Describe the format you use to develop a lesson plan.
11. What should schools do for students?
12. Is the teaching of content important? Why? Why not?
13. How do you handle the different ability levels of students?
14. How do you account for the affective domain in your teaching?
15. How would your students describe you?
16. In what professional organizations do you hold membership?

17. Why did you choose the teaching profession?
18. How have you recently improved your professional skills?
19. What is the toughest aspect of teaching today?
20. What is the role of homework?
21. What was your most positive experience while student teaching? Negative?
22. What activities would you be willing to sponsor if you are hired for this position?
23. Could a student of low academic ability receive a high grade in your class?
24. What is your system for evaluating student work?
25. What is your philosophy of education? Music education?
26. How would you handle a student who is a consistent behavioral problem in your class?
27. What five words would you use to describe yourself?
28. What are your strengths? Weaknesses?
29. What provisions would you make for a gifted student?
30. What would a visitor in your class see?
31. How would you communicate student progress to parents?
32. Define a superior teacher.
33. What is your opinion of holding students after school for detention?
34. Do you like laughter in your classroom?
35. What is the role of the student within your classroom?
36. Describe an assignment you gave to your students while student teaching.
37. Are you well organized?
38. A student tells you he/she is experimenting with drugs. What do you do?
39. How would you change the public school system?
40. What do you like most about being a teacher?
41. Which aspects of teaching do you like least?
42. Do you want your students to like you?
43. How do you cope with stress?
44. How would you involve parents in the learning process?
45. Can a school be too student-oriented? Explain.
46. Why should I hire you?

47. What questions have I not asked that you wished I would have raised?
48. If you are selected for this position what can we do to help you be successful?
49. Tell me about yourself.
50. What is the role of a building principal?

Reprinted by permission from the September 1983 issue of the *NASSP* [National Association of Secondary School Principals] *Bulletin*, Copyright.

FOLLOW–UP CORRESPONDENCE

A thank-you letter should be drafted immediately following the invitation to interview. Upon completion of the interview, refine the letter by personalizing it and immediately mail a copy to each person who was involved in the process. This shows the employer that you are organized and have a continued interest in the position. A well written follow–up letter will only enhance your chances of getting the job.

Bradley A. Johnson

319 Meadowlark Lane, Apt. 14 C
Royal Heights, Missouri 64801
(417) 625-0000 home

June 3, 199_

Mr. Thomas E. Davis
Principal, Royal Heights High School
1485 Newman Road
Royal Heights, MO 64801

Dear Mr. Davis:

First paragraph. Thank them for the interview and express your appreciation for the courtesy and consideration extended. State the date of the meeting and the position you interviewed for.

Second paragraph. Reaffirm your interest in the job. Mention a specific aspect of the interview that you found impressive. Perhaps it was well organized or the school facilities were outstanding. Find a way to compliment their efforts.

Final paragraph. Close with a suggestion for further action, such as your availability for an additional interview at their convenience. Offer appended information and a willingness to supply added references. Thank them for their continued consideration of your application.

Sincerely,

Bradley A. Johnson

Once you have accepted a position, pen a brief letter of appreciation to all who helped you attain this goal (references, friends, family, etc.). This follow–up correspondence is a professional courtesy. A draft is presented below.

Bradley A. Johnson

319 Meadowlark Lane, Apt. 14 C
Royal Heights, Missouri 64801
(417) 625-0000 home

June 10, 199_

Dear Dr. Carnine,

Just a short note to thank you for serving as a reference for me during my job search. I recently accepted a position as Director of Bands at Royal Heights Community School, Royal Heights, Missouri. Again, my sincere thanks for your assistance and support.

Sincerely yours,

Bradley A. Johnson

If you are not open to promoting creativity to all of your students, then you become a limited instuctor who has allowed traditionalism to impede contemporary thought. However, with an understanding of the relationship between musicality and the educational process, you can better offer your students the opportunity to search for the music "within and beyond".

— Phillip C. Wise, Ph.D.

APPENDIX

A. Administrative Forms

B. Publishers

C. Professional Organizations

D. Professional Journals

APPENDIX A

ADMINISTRATIVE FORMS

Many of you have heard the saying *work smart – not hard.* The following section will assist you in this endeavor. Feel free to copy these forms or use them as guides to create your own.

Record of Achievement
Student Health Registration
Identification Card
Financial Obligation Form
Rehearsal Planner
Band Report
Complimentary Report
Checkout Record
Student Personnel File
Percussion Assignments
Educational Trips
Transportation Release Form
Audition Form
Challenge Adjudication Form
Festival Evaluation
Lesson Plan Outline For Literature Discussion
Instrument Checkout & Repair Record
Instructional Lesson Record
Teaching Schedule A
Teaching Schedule B
Discipline Record

RECORD OF ACHIEVEMENT

Sunday	Monday	Tuesday	Wednesday	Thursday	Friday	Saturday

STUDENT HEALTH REGISTRATION

Student Name _____ SS# _____

Address _____ Date of Birth _____

Contact Person Name _____

Contact Person Address _____

Describe the following: (use back page if necessary)

recent illness _____

chronic or long-term illness _____

allergies _____

medicines currently being taken _____

other medical or physical restrictions _____
_____
_____
_____

Parent or Guardian Consent Statement

I grant permission for the above named person to be treated and/or hospitalized by a licensed physician if an emergency situation arises.

SIGNED: _____ DATE: _____

WORK PHONE: _____ HOME PHONE: _____

IDENTIFICATION CARD

Name _____ Address _____

Parent(s)/Guardian(s) Name _____

Home Phone _____ Secondary Phone No. _____

Grade ___ Age ___ Instrument _____ Years Played _____

Lesson Book _____ Private Study   yes   no

Additional Information:

FINANCIAL OBLIGATION FORM

Name _____ Date _____

The following financial obligation(s) is to be entered on the above person's business office record.

Description   **Cost**

Music _____

Lesson Book _____

Accessories _____

Instrument Rental Fee _____

Instrument Repair _____

Uniform Fee _____

Item(s) Not Returned _____

Other _____

                          Total Amount _____

Please remit to the Royal Heights High School Business Office

cc: student

REHEARSAL PLANNER

Date _____

Composition	Page	Measure	Work Needed	Comments

BAND REPORT

Date _____

Grade _____ Homeroom _____

Counselor _____

Dear Parent(s)/Guardian(s):

I feel you should know that _____
is presently doing unsatisfactory work in band.

Comments:

The student has been advised that this notice is being sent. If you
feel a meeting could in any way help improve _____
work, phone the school office at _____
to arrange a meeting.

_____
Director of Bands

cc: counselor, file

COMPLIMENTARY REPORT

Student Name _____ Date _____

Subject _____ Director _____

Academic Comments:

____ Scores high on examinations
____ Works to the best of ability
____ Has developed good study habits
____ Uses extra time to increase depth and understanding of
     music
____ Is sincerely trying to do better

Behavioral Comments:

____ Shows leadership in band activities
____ Helps fellow students and cooperates with director
____ Works well independently
____ Demonstrates self–discipline
____ Has shown improvement in classroom behavior

Additional comments:

_____

Director of Bands

CHECKOUT RECORD

Name	Item	Date Out	Date In

STUDENT PERSONNEL FILE

_____   _____
Student   Date

                                    _____
_____   Sem./Qtr.

Comments

Musical progress

_____

Work habits

_____

Social adjustments and peer relationships

_____

Interests, aptitudes, and abilities

_____

Interaction with teacher(s) and staff

_____

Health or emotional concerns

_____

Response to class rules and procedures

_____

Additional comments:

PERCUSSION ASSIGNMENTS

Ensemble _____

Composition _____

Name	Snare	Bass	Timpani	Cymbals	Bells	Triangle	Other

EDUCATIONAL TRIPS

During the year, your child will have the opportunity to take educational trips to various places both in and outside of the community. A signed permission form is required for instrumental faculty to allow your child to participate in all 19__ - 19__ educational trips.

Please return this form to the instrumental music department
by _____ .

_____

Parent(s)/Guardian(s) Signature

_____

Name of Student

_____

Date

TRANSPORTATION RELEASE FORM

_____ has permission to ride home with
Student

_____ from _____
Name/Relation   Event

on_____ .
        Date

I accept all transportation responsibility and will not hold the Royal
Heights Community School District responsible for any accident
or injury incurred during this return ride home.

_____   _____
Parent/Guardian   Date

_____   _____
Parent/Guardian   Date

BAND AUDITION FORM

NAME _____ INSTRUMENT _____

60 Points Possible	Comments	Score
Scales (10)		
Tone (10)		
Articulation (10)		
Musicality/Phrasing (10)		
Sightreading (if applicable) Etude/Solo (10)		
Rhythm (10)		

TOTAL _____

Comments:

CHALLENGE ADJUDICATION FORM

DATE _____ INSTRUMENT _____

60 Points Possible	Comments	#1	#2
Scales (10)			
Tone (10)			
Articulation (10)			
Musicality/Phrasing (10)			
Sightreading (if applicable) Etude/Solo (10)			
Rhythm (10)			

TOTAL _____   _____

Comments:

FESTIVAL EVALUATION

_____
Name   Date

Tone quality. When students play, do you hear expressive tone qualities? Describe these sounds. Did you hear any vibrato?

_____
_____
_____
_____

Intonation. Did students tune before playing? If so, what approach did they use? Did the ensemble play in tune?

_____
_____
_____
_____

Balance and blend. Did the ensemble blend well or did certain parts stick out? Could the melody or solo parts be heard?

_____
_____
_____
_____

Articulation. Did students articulate clearly and together?

_____
_____
_____
_____

Attacks, releases, and phrases. Did students enter and release at the same time?   Did the ensemble phrase together?

_____

_____

_____

_____

Control of tempo and dynamic range.   Were the students able to maintain tempos? Did the ensemble perform with a wide range of dynamics?

_____

_____

_____

_____

Rhythmic and technical accuracy. Was the performance free of wrong notes and rhythms?

_____

_____

_____

_____

General musicianship. Were the students dressed appropriately for a public performance? Did they have good posture, instrument position, and hand position? Did they do something while performing that you have never seen or heard before?

_____

_____

_____

_____

Additional Comments:

LESSON PLAN OUTLINE
FOR LITERATURE DISCUSSION

DATE _____ SEMESTER _____ CLASS _____

COMPOSITION _____

COMPOSER _____

PERIOD/DATE: _____

COMPOSER'S IMPORTANCE: _____

BACKGROUND: _____

FORM: _____

STYLE: _____

TEXTURE: _____

COMPOSITIONAL
TECHNIQUES: _____

OTHER:

INSTRUMENT CHECKOUT
& REPAIR RECORD

Instrument	Make	Serial No.	Issued To	Date	Date Returned	Repair Needed

INSTRUCTIONAL LESSON RECORD

Name _____ Instrument _____

Date	Lesson Assignment	Comments	Grade
1			
2			
3			
4			
5			
6			
7			
8			
9			
10			
11			
12			
13			
14			

TEACHING SCHEDULE A

	Monday	Tuesday	Wednesday	Thursday	Friday
Time Subject					
Time Subject					
Time Subject					
Time Subject					
Time Subject					
Time Subject					
Time Subject					
Time Subject					
Time Subject					
Time Subject					
Time Subject					

Teaching Schedule B

Hour	Monday	Tuesday	Wednesday	Thursday	Friday	Saturday

DISCIPLINE RECORD

Date	Student Name	Rule Broken	Consequence	Follow-Up

APPENDIX B

PUBLISHERS

Alfred Publishing Company, Inc.
16380 Roscoe Boulevard, P.O. Box 10003
Van Nuys, California 91408

Arrangers' Publishing Company
200 Hill Avenue, Suite Four
Nashville, Tennessee 37214

B & B Music Publications
P.O. Box 9492
Moscow, Idaho 83843

Big Hill Music Press
P.O. Box 278
Grand Coteau, Louisiana 70541

Boosey & Hawkes, Inc.
52 Cooper Square
New York, New York 10003

Bourne International Music Co.
5 West 37th Street
New York, New York 10003

Carl Fischer, Inc.
62 Cooper Square
New York, New York 10003

Claude T. Smith Publications
18850 West 116th Street
Olathe, Kansas 66061

C.L. Barnhouse Company
Box 680
Oskaloosa, Iowa 52577

David E. Smith Publications
4826 Shabbona Road
Deckerville, Michigan 48427

Doug Beach Music
P.O. Box 278
Delevan, New York 14042

Edwin F. Kalmus & Co. Inc.
6403 West Rogers Circle
Boca Raton, Florida 33432

Grand Mesa Music Publishers
1038 Chipeta Avenue
Grand Junction, Colorado 81501

Hal Leonard Corporation
7777 West Bluemound Road, P.O. Box 13819
Milwaukee, Wisconsin 53213

Heritage Music Press
501 East Third Street, P.O. Box 802
Dayton, Ohio 45401

Kendor Music Inc.
P.O. Box 278
Delevan, New York 14042-0278

Manhattan Beach Music
1595 East 46th Street
Brooklyn, New York 11234-3122

Marina Music Service Inc.
P.O. Box 46159
Seattle, Washington 98126

Neil A. Kjos Music Company
4380 Jutland Drive, P.O. Box 178270
San Diego, California 92177

Phoebus Publications
1303 Faust Avenue
Oshkosh, Wisconsin 54901

Queenwood Publications
11101 East Mercer Lane
Scottsdale, Arizona 85251

Shawnee Press Inc.
49 Waring Drive
Delaware Gap, Pennsylvania 18327

Sierra Music Publications
Box 543
Liberty Lake, Washington 99019

Southern Music Company
P.O. Box 329
San Antonio, Texas 78206

TRN Music Publisher
P.O. Box 1076
Ruidoso, New Mexico 88345

Walrus Music Publishing
P.O. Box 11267
Glendale, California 91209

Warner Brothers/CPP/Belwin Inc.
15800 Northwest 48th Avenue, P.O. Box 4340
Miami, Florida 33014

William Allen Music Inc.
P.O. Box 790
Newington, Virginia 22122

Wingert-Jones Music Inc.
2026 Broadway, Box 419878
Kansas City, Missouri 64100

This listing is not all-inclusive.

APPENDIX C

PROFESSIONAL ORGANIZATIONS

American Bandmasters Association
Richard Thurston, Secretary-Treasurer
1521 South Pickard
Norman, Oklahoma 73069

American School Band Directors Association
James Hewitt, Office Manager
P.O. Box 146
Otsego, Michigan 49078

Association for Technology in Music Instruction
Peter Webster
School of Music, Northwestern University
Evanston, Illinois 60200

Christian Instrumental Directors Association
David Smith, Membership Chairman
4826 Shabbona Road
Deckerville, Michigan 48427

Conductors' Guild, Inc.
Judy Ann Voois, Administrative Director
103 South High Street, Room 6
West Chester, Pennsylvania 19380

The International Association of Jazz Educators
William Lee, Executive Director
Box 724
Manhattan, Kansas 66502

Music Educators National Conference
Elizabeth Lasko
1806 Robert Fulton Drive
Reston, Virginia 22070

National Band Association
Valerie Brown
P.O. Box 121292
Nashville, Tennessee 37200

National Catholic Band Association
John Dunphy
305 Maple Avenue
Wyncote, Pennsylvania 19095

Women Band Directors National Association
Patricia Root, President
M.T.S.U. Bands, Box 63
Murfreesboro, Tennessee 37130

The World Association of Symphonic Bands and Ensembles
Egil Gundersen, Treasurer
Ronningjordet 21, N-3718
Skien, Norway

This listing is not all-inclusive.

APPENDIX D

PROFESSIONAL JOURNALS

Bandworld
407 Terrace Street
Ashland, Oregon 97520

BD [Band Directors] Guide
2533 South Maple Avenue #102
Tempe, Arizona 85282

The Instrumentalist
200 Northfield Road
Northfield, Illinois 60093

Jazz Educators Journal
Box 724
Manhattan, Kansas 66505

Journal of Music Teacher Education
Journal of Research in Music Education
Music Educators Journal
Teaching Music
1806 Robert Fulton Drive
Reston, Virginia 22091-4348

This listing is not all-inclusive.

REFERENCES

Austin, James. "Meaningful Contests." *The Instrumentalist* 48 (November 1993): 77, 80.

Besson, Malcolm E., Alphouse M. Tatarunis, and Samuel L. Forcucci. *Teaching Music In Today's Secondary Schools.* New York, NY: Holt, Rinehart and Winston, 1980.

Cantor, Lee, and Marlene Cantor. *Assertive Discipline.* Santa Monica, CA: Lee Cantor & Associates, 1992.

Christensen, Joe, and Gil Lettow, eds. *Iowa Bandmaster Assistance Program For Young and Prospective Teachers.* Des Moines, IA: Iowa Association of Music Dealers, 1991.

Dean, Robert, ed. *An Administrator's Guide To Curriculum.* Cedar Falls, IA: The University of Northern Iowa, 1990.

Del Borgo, Elliot. "Band or Wind Ensemble - An Important Distinction." *The Instrumentalist* 39 (November 1984): 94.

Diekman, J.R. *Get Your Message Across.* Belmond, CA: Prentice-Hall, Inc., 1979.

Ferguson, James E. "Interviewing Teacher Candidates: 100 Questions To Ask." *NASSP* [National Association of Secondary School Principals] *Bulletin* (May 1983): 118-120.

Foxman, Loretta D. *The Executive Resume Book.* Crockett, TX: Wiley & Sons, Inc., 1989.

Gifford, Robert M. "Alternative Seating Solutions." *The Instrumentalist* 49 (April 1995): 16-22, 27, 88.

Hindsley, Mark H. "Seating Arrangements for Concert Band." *The Instrumentalist* 31 (May 1976): 17.

Hoffer, Charles R. *Teaching Music In The Secondary Schools.* Belmont, CA: Wadsworth Inc., 1991.

Hoffer, Margorie. "How To Practice." *NSOA* [National School Orchestra Association] *Bulletin* 35 (April 1993): 1, 3.

Kuzmich, John, and Lee Bash. *Instrumental Jazz Instruction.* West Nyack, NY: Parker Inc., 1984.

McKee, M. Max. "Stop Doing That." *Bandworld* (August – October 189): 16.

Rosaker, Marcia, ed. *Design Yourself.* LeMars, IA: Westmar University Press, 1995.

Security Mutual Life Nebraska. "Personal Staff Development - Being A Professional." *The Mutualog.* Original source unknown.

Smith, Norman, and Albert Stoutamire. *Band Music Notes.* San Diego, CA: Kjos West – Neil A Kjos Jr., Publisher, 1979.

Wise, Phillip C. "The Musical Experience - A Guide for Parents." *The Iowa Music Educator* 49 (February 1996): 36-37.

Wise, Phillip C. "Self-Inflicted Burnout." Parts 1, 2. *Bandworld* 11 (March-April 1996): 13 (May-June 1996): 13.

Wise, Phillip C. and Wise, Terry S. "The Dragon Tamer's Guide." *Learning* (September-October 1996)